RELEASED INTO THE WILD

by
Beth Ann Bassein
with artwork and photography by Linda Wolfe,
Charles H. Smith, and others

To order additional copies of this book, contact:
Xlibris Corporation
1-888-795-4274
www.Xlibris.com
Orders@Xlibris.com

This work is not directly connected with that commendable endeavor of nursing sick and injured wildlife back to health and releasing them into their natural habitat. Rather it is about finding release from a locked-in pattern of existence that allows no time to experience the natural world. It is about finding new and rewarding interests in all aspects of nature and coming to a greater determination to do no harm as we find respite there.

This work is dedicated to all environmentally conscious people who open our awareness to the values and pleasures of moving into our delicate and fragile out-of-doors.

CONTENTS

I. RELEASED INTO THE WILD

Freed from anxiety by the hope that my life will take a different turn, I enthusiastically pull away from twenty-five years teaching college students the jewels of British and American literature. At first I dream of doing nothing I have ever done before. Deeply grooved habits developed over twenty-five years soon dispel this dream, but by reconnecting with my early life, finding people with inclinations similar to mine, and utilizing a therapy I have always used, that of writing down my pre-occupations, I manage to escape the professor's captivity with ease. Because teaching at Southern Colorado State has been strenuous, I assume I have built-up stamina waiting to be utilized. I am not a caged bird that cannot be released into the wild. Making friends with a bull snake and walking down a road beside a green-tailed towhee are not things I've had time to do when tied to my teaching schedule, but now, it's "Wait up, here I come."

A closet birdwatcher for most of my teaching career, I stifle my desire to find good birding spots. Telling a friend of this deprivation, I explain that yes, there are flies, gnats, skunks. Birds do let loose on heads sometimes, but if you are born near the woods, make hollyhock dolls as well as mud pies, you don't worry about those living their lives close to dirt. Rather, you yearn to find out more about everything in the out-of-doors. I tell her living outside has always been my notion of a life well spent, that I trailed along with brothers who fished, poked in the weeds where there were black snakes, built bowers of willows that sheltered streams with turtles. I tell her I even grew up taking walks by myself. I also grew up pulling weeds in a big garden, picking blackberries to put under sugar for my early morning breakfast before others were up, and working in fields, when my brothers went off to war. Realizing, when signing off on a twenty-five year career, that I am getting back in the grooves of childhood does not deter my push forward. I am in my element.

With surprise, I learn that retirees in the United States are the most cared-for segment of society. Opportunities to find employment, entertainment, new experiences traveling, and volunteering are everywhere. When I discover the Parks Department of El Paso County in Colorado offers endless chances to get into the wild, I am amazed. Going for a hike, looking for birds and other wildlife, and helping kids see the value of these natural things have always been the sole responsibility of individuals occasionally enjoying an outdoor weekend, not the Parks Department, or so I think. To discover expert leaders promoting nature as the focus of their career, and getting paid for it by county governments, is a revelation. Previously operating in an English Department on a limited budget, I marvel that there are funds available to equip and operate nature centers for the benefit of the community.

Amazed I am, but very pleased. Here is a chance to glean from people interested in the same things I am, to take part in organized activities in the out-of-doors, and to come to know these subjects, about which I have limited understanding. Looking more closely at a daisy or horsemint, listening to bull frogs croak, standing still while deer feed, and finding people who count birds -- all are indulgences I haven't had enough time for before.

Add to the above the benefits and pleasures of reading Edward Abbey, David Quammen, Annie Dillard, Barbara Kingsolver, Ann Zwinger, and a host of others who are speaking to the important issue of preservation of natural resources, and life becomes even richer and more purposeful. Actually these naturalists are adding to what Wordsworth, Coleridge, even Keats, Shelley, and Byron impressed upon me so long ago, when my head fairly danced with their verse about the world they cherished. Here is a renewed chance to narrow the gap between idealism and what lies at my fingertips. Here is a chance to revisit the real meaning of Wordsworth's "O world, I cannot get thee close enough, thy winds, thy wide grey skies, thy mists that roll and rise," lines that were lodged in my head when I was young and impressionable.

Even with recurring thoughts that, after all our efforts, after all our protective legislation, the natural world will go down to bombings, bulldozers, pollution, and political gain, I cannot dwell on lost hope long. I seek places free of automobile noise, television, the smell of gas. I run away to places of comfort and renewal.

Moving out of the cage teaching puts around me, of course, can do little to alter my writing obsession. No resolution, like saying I will do nothing I have ever done before, can annihilate this passion. My therapy, my release from whatever nags me, my healer of frustrations -- who would want to throw this to the wind? To spin out a poem, think it is good, even if the next day it is nonsense, or write a few sentences that please, is a tremendously satisfying exercise. The morning is not lost when this compulsion is in play. One even imagines one is doing good. As I am soon to find out, to write about a bird, a flower, or a child looking closely at a butterfly is to re-live experience, understand and enjoy it with more depth, to hold it closer and longer.

The selections in Section One deal initially with the pull nature has on us. Section Two is about those particular places in the wild which we enjoy, that pull us to them again and again. Moving deeper into specific phenomena, the next three sections result from going beyond the quick look at a plant or animal, where exclamations over their appeal are the most usual response, to specifics about each. Many pieces in these sections result from enjoying what others have written that enhance special attributes of each plant or creature. Section Six underscores observations made because of the changes taking place from season to season. All these essays and poems result from ruminations and investigations that come about because I take time to experience the natural world. Interestingly, the interests of people who have lent their artistic and photographic talents to this volume parallel mine in numerous respects.

STEPPING OUTSIDE

Take a walk, and you are a changed person. You are less awkward. You are not bumping into chairs. You may not have bathed, but you are suddenly clean. You know the dirt you'll encounter will not be human dirt, except for the occasional ravine filled with trash. And that you will ignore, because you've gained power over irritants. Something is about to happen that you will remember. Will you see the first bluebird of March? Sense the texture of bark, where a brown creeper is descending, or a rock on which a dipper bobs? The moment we open our senses to what is before us, say, ah ha, this moment enters our memory to be lodged for our keeping.

Garden of the Gods. Colorado Springs.
Photo: Jane G. Smith

Mention horse trails, and I think Garden of the Gods, where 200 pinyon jays flocked on an October afternoon in 1963, flocked where I was riding tandem through scrub oak and juniper. Had my horse known, it could have slipped me and run, I was so into the pinyon blue decorating gnarled and dull-green junipers. Mention pinyon jays and that scene bobs into my consciousness.

When we step into the out-of-doors, an uncanny power takes over. We are open, strong, unmindful of monotony. Dents in us are easily made. But there is more to it. When I released a female robin tangled in nylon fishing cord at the ponds in Fountain Creek Regional Park, when I closed my hand over its eyes, hurried to my car where there were clippers to cut the cord I could not break, the cord drawing a ring of blood from the robin's leg, something else happened. When I was helped by a fisherman with clippers in hand, when I set the bird free, I witnessed a power I had not experienced before. Not just my power to envy and admire, to help nature, to redress the carelessness of dropping tangled nylon string, but the power of the bird to shoot into the sky with a force unmatchable in myself. This survival driven bird was re-enacting the universal that all living things, including humans, have at the very basis of their existence.

Watercolor of Robin by Linda Wolfe

I sensed the power in this bird, and I connected. Moving into nature is to connect, then disconnect, go away carrying more than we carried before. Because we can only look at the uncanny, the powerful, the beautiful momentarily, we need the patience required to give it our closest scrutiny when it happens to emblazon itself before us. Patience and memory, are they not at the heart of our most fulfilling experiences?

Where better to connect and disconnect than when I arrive to find the poets in my Baca lodge in a fret because a swallow bobs against our high ceiling trying to get out. With everyone, it is "What to do?" None of my friends know. Nor do I, but I am soon to find out. Pivoting on the hiatus of first arrival, not ready to unpack or manage the practical, I walk under the swallow, look up and utter the same distress as my friends. It flies down and lands on a table. I put my hand over its back, carry it gently to the door, so excited, yet so calm, that I feel nothing except the incredibly soft silkiness of its back in my palm. I deny myself closer inspection. I do not look down at the bird. All I want is its freedom. When it flies, my sense of well-being reaches a peak it has not reached before. The bird is released into the wild, and so are my friends and myself.

Like with the robin there was great physical stamina in this graceful swallow. And dare I hope, a little trust?

If you want to add substance to the least structured, most aimless day of the week, you may want to let nature do it. During summer on Sundays, try the creekbottom trail off 26th Street at Bear Creek Regional Park. The whites, pinks, lavenders, and blues of the wildflowers will tether you, as you move to the corner of the park and to a higher elevation. If you can tear yourself away from the manifold leaf shapes and moments of color, you will search the trees overhead for the vireo that can't stop calling. Rising higher, Indian paint brush will glue you to its flame for as long as you can take the stimulus. With the early morning sun as a spotlight, you can give it your close attention. "I got ya, you can't take your eyes off me," it seems to say.

Indian Paintbrush. Photo: El Passo County Parks Staff

Pulling yourself away from this color, you move on until you run into a cluster of six of these firebrands. Again you are caught, hooked into an inescapable mode, one you didn't bring to the park. Luck coming your way, three American goldfinches in their brightest summer colors will close out this image and bring more of nature's seductive lure. Back at the nature center, a lone mule deer will fill you with "ohs" and "ahs" where any "whys" and "why nots" have been. You will be softened into a morning of receptiveness.

Fountain Creek Park will do the same for you. Visualize watching a mother turtle display egg laying at your feet. Feel along with her as she carves out a bit of a ditch in a hard, compacted trail; wait for her as she tries to dislodge next summer's offspring. Moreover, sit at the reception desk all morning as a volunteer, while walker after walker comes in to report the turtle's progress. Experience the moment when one walker answers your "How's she getting on?" with "She's back in the water." By now, your interest is definitely maternal, as is that of the visitor.

And, yes, three different batches of orioles are enough to color any morning, day, or week. And if you want total release from whatever glues you to the part of the past you'd as soon be rid of, study wood ducks at the first pond. Live with them as long as you can hold them in your binoculars, and return to them again as you test your capacity to explain to a visitor from Germany, who doesn't speak much English, why there are boxes on stakes in some of the ponds. Of course, to keep the momentum of your enthusiasm at a high pitch, watch the great blue heron pace steadily through the water with its eyes on a fish and its beak pointed. You'll step forward as judiciously, come Monday.

Hazards should not deter. That occasional unleashed dog which always barks at strangers or its master/mistress who has never let anybody tell him/her what to do are not prevalent enough to discourage walks in the parks. Sometimes, however, they encourage me to take another path, to listen for the ripple of the creek or the downward spiral of the call of a red-tailed hawk in a less traveled area. Deer season and the blast-happy poacher who took one of Bear Creek's most prized inhabitants make a bear seem timid, as a hindrance to quiet meditative strolls. Most days, however, there are only nice sounds: a chickadee communicating with members of its clan, a quacking duck, or the scuttling of leaves - no exploding guns. Getting acquainted with local parks may lead to an expansiveness that will take you on journeys you never dreamed could be so interesting.

The highways prove hazardless as Dodie Hiatt, Betty Boyd, Marge Abbott, and I drive to Socorro, New Mexico, to the crane festival in November. Had we taken a longer route, we would have missed a splendid pond beside the highway, where a half dozen varieties of winter ducks paddled and dunked. These, of course, were mere appetizers to the sumptuous and elegant banquet at the Bosque del Apache, where some 75,000 sandhills, snow geese, and assorted ducks filled the wetlands with their tantalizingly wonderful calls.

Anyone going there should wait around until evening for the gracing of the golden sunset against the mountains by the flocks returning from the fields - this is a once-in-a-lifetime experience! And by day, look close for the preening cormorants - what contentment as they meet winter's subdued demands! I also have a particular affection for big healthy turkeys parting the leaves for dropped acorns. "Mind your own business, and I'll mind mine," they seem to say. I like how they turkey their way over ridges.

THE PRIMITIVE PULSE

The mountains have places
I like to return to, alone.
Going there with close friends
because there are berries
only entices me to walk out early,
before others are up, and glide
up a familiar trail, never stopping
to inspect a twig or flower,
just letting the air float me
in among bird calls,
the motionless brace of a mule deer,
the slant of the sun's rays.
A peculiar coolness bathes me
like the breath of an angel
my father let down
when we strode over acres
he'd never plow.

II. RETURNING TO A CERTAIN GROVE

I confess "the human spirit" and "the American spirit" are too elusive to have much meaning for me. "Spirit of Place," however, is quite to the point, as I touch base with locales I have own. The spring in the hillside in Missouri with water like no other I've ever tasted, the road where we saw the pile of snakes in Virginia, the slope below my brother's home in Brush Prairie, Washington (before it was developed), the west hillside in Woodland Park, Colorado, where I see all the way to Breckenridge, the Jungle Lodge in Costa Rica, where I saw the Trogon and listened to howler monkeys in early morning, that fast food place in Socorro where Lois Hayna and I sat in awe looking at a double rainbow, the ruddy turnstones in a meadow on Molokai, the rooks outside Moscow, the sunbirds on a vine over the front porch in India -- all these are locked in my memory and sneak into my musings without much prompting.

Our parks with their nature centers flush out my collection of places which take on a sharpness that causes memory to clutch and hold. The actual buildings at Bear Creek and Fountain Creek parks are special places because within the walls, there is a remarkable unity of purpose -- to open minds to our dependence on nature, the joy to be found in it, and the need to protect it for future generations. Their work is made easier by the availability of nature's bounty in the parks: if they mention dogbane, they can point it out as they conduct hikes.

Beyond the actual buildings and the people who work in them, there are the trails and their special attractions. Even the spot, where I looked through the scrub oak to see a coyote, is lodged in my memory along with pockets in the trees, where what I saw peeking through was a deer, that soon moved on. Or on the trail where I suddenly feel, until I hear the freight train way over to your

Dogbane Photo. Charles H. Smith

right, that I am totally alone, or only a bit farther, the place where we saw the tiny garter snake atop a teasel, or on around the corner where the asparagus keeps getting more plentiful -- these are spots as familiar as my living room. Clear too, is the place where I always see a song sparrow. How is it that the spot where you first identify a bird takes on as much significance as the bird itself?

Yes, places add a rich texture to most people's lives. But I am forgetting there are places I avoid -- the one where a car missed mine by only two inches, the office building where I became an expert at tabulating J. S. Lerner Vogue's sales of bras, panties, slips; and other tedious jobs all those hot summers working my way through college. These are places I would like to forget. Thankfully, they lose their distastefulness as they compete with ones experienced in the natural world.

Coming to Baca in May nearly every year since 1991, I still know it only superficially. Yet I feel its presence immediately upon arriving and long after leaving. The quietness, the expansiveness across the flat valley to the west and the incredible beauty of the mountains to the east make an indelible impression. I sink into its solemnity, its magic, find release and rest there.

Baca, as we affectionately call it, is a portion of the old Baca Land Grant that encompassed much of the San Luis Valley, an area larger than the state of Rhode Island, but which has been subdivided and is now in the possession

Baca,
Near Colorado College's
San Luis Valley Campus.
Photo: Beth Ann Bassein

of various owners. Colorado College of Colorado Springs is lucky to have acquired the acres they call their second campus, lucky because classes in many fields come for study -- biology, geology, southwest studies, creative writing -- and lucky to have the land, which they will not develop beyond the lodges used for students, while there for relatively short periods.

I have been fortunate to come to Baca through programs conducted by Colorado College, private trips, and writing retreats. I know Baca superficially because there is so much to know. The lay of the land, including the drainage of snow water from the high peaks to the east, the water level, the salt accumulations in the soil, are all subjects for study. Lectures by the dozens could be given on its geology, including signs of the wearing down of the peaks. The history of the farms is rich. The Sand Dunes to the south are of great interest. The valley's vegetation and water are sufficient to support abundant wildlife,

Sandhill Cranes, San Luis Valley.
Photo: Charles H. Smith

some even feeding off the surrounding land used for grazing and farming, the large sandhill crane population wintering in the area among others.

My first encounter with the area took place when I came with a group led by professors from Colorado College. With Joe Gordon leading us in a nature writing exercise, I revisited an old botany assignment that I had dealt with superficially at a previous time. (After all, I was an English major!) I learned from Joe that if you really want to know a thing, you have to look at it piece by piece, part by part. "Take that mullein there. Tell us what it is" was a daunting task, for such an exercise takes the participant into and beyond beauty, texture, symmetry, weathering, and reproductive organs. I never look at any plant the same way again. And I realize that every living plant, every living creature, has a similarly complicated and intriguing story like this woolly "weed."

Subsequent stays at Baca have allowed me to rest, write, wander. Of the people I've met there, not one has told me anything but good things about the area. What I carry with me most intensely from these visits comes from morning and afternoon walks. Mountain bluebirds are at the top of my grand experiences, but green-tailed towhees, yellow-rumped warblers, meadowlarks, high flying red-tailed hawks, herds of deer, and many other creatures spell Baca's lure. Elk can be seen in the area. Walk into near-by Crestone and add pinyon jays and western tanagers to the list.

Coming there in May 2002 for a three-day stay with a writing group, I was saddened to see the creeks with no water in them, all absolutely bone dry. As unusual as it seemed, I had to conclude that this favorite spot, after all, was part of Colorado, which was suffering the worst drought in decades and subsequently extremely destructive fires. The year before we had been lulled to sleep by the sound of the cold water speeding off the snow-laden mountains to the east. My first short walk netted nothing but robins and magpies, the perennial put-up-with-anything friends. I did marvel at several morning cloaks and other small blue butterflies. Although there were carpets of golden banner, it seemed not as robust as years before. Everything kept reminding me that all Colorado was crying for rain. The land seemed a kindling box, the grasses a faded tan. I wanted to find hubcaps to put out drinking water. At the beginning of my first full day there, I set out on my early morning walk to discover if the drought had driven all the wildlife away, and the migrating birds had just decided not to stop.

Forgetting it takes a while to find what lurks under the ground cover and behind leafed-out trees, I at first can hear only one distant meadowlark. But when I head west I hear the sweet song of the green-tailed towhee. Yes, I am right, I detect its rufous cap with my binoculars. (On my return, I walk on one side of the road while the same towhee walks at the other side -- the two of us in tandem, you might say. You can't do better than that!) In the same area, I spot a white-crowned sparrow and begin to hear not one, but numerous, meadowlarks.

Sketch of Butterflies by Linda Wolfe.

13

I take advantage of the green area where birds congregate near a small overflow from the Baca property's sewage ponds. But before I arrive there, I spot two flocks of deer, numbering all together ten. Magpies are out, as are robins. A cottontail hops across the path in front of me. At the ponds, geese call, ducks make their exit, swallows dart over water, kill deer give their alarm call. And, lo, in the high trees near the seepage area, house wrens come through with their fussy little prattle. A little farther along, a flycatcher darts out for an insect.

The drought is upon us, but we are not deserted. The wildlife is making the most of it, resorting to measures they haven't needed before. The deer, I know, are eating a lot of hay instead of green sprouts. I move on to where I saw the mountain blue bird last year. Although my voyeuristic gaze does not net me this prize, I remember there will be another day. Perhaps tomorrow, before heading back to civilization. As I return to my writing desk in one of the Baca lodges, people tell me they are hearing some unbelievable bird songs.

Four days into marathon TV watching that followed 9-11, I turn myself over to Baca. I am stymied at not knowing what to think or how to cope. Calling my daughters can scarcely help, except to know what I already know, that they are safe. I feel I cannot go on wanting to get on with life in face of so much death. My head is cluttered with horror and the *perfectness* of the crime. People are dead and dying. The killers are no more. Detectives have no work to do. Lawyers have no criminals to defend. Any response cannot get at the heart of the matter. Do they hate us? Of course, they do. Our luxurious living, our need for oil, our support of Israel, our know-it-all stance can arouse nothing but envy and hate. Maybe after my lifetime, there will be remedies, but now bombs will only compound the issue.

Taking a walk at the Baca campus rescues me. After a twenty-four hour stay with my night spent in a valley Bed and Breakfast, I come home anxious but much relieved. I had found release in the wild.

HER ROYAL HIGHNESS

Pikes Peak is not quite the same as she was when we arrived in Colorado Springs. We know she is eroding; we know roads, lightning, rains, snows, and long periods of dryness alter this mountain, all 14,110 feet of her. Many of us, however, are unconscious of these changes, unless we work on the mountain as custodians of roads, forests, or tourist stops. Or, unless we are skiers and hikers. We mostly view her and respond to her mystical allure from a distance. And we do tend to forget her majesty.

She is the picture in the frame of our windows, but she is much more. From our splendid vantage point in Colorado Springs, we do discern changes from morning to night and those wrought by storm and wind. We've all seen her pink glow in the morning, the sun hitting her before it engulfs us. We've marveled at this remarkable phenomenon. "Pink mountain? You must be still asleep!" outsiders croak. We who are acquainted with her many secrets know her Royal Highness is merely flush after a good night's sleep.

When this preliminary glow subsides, her rocks and crevices do not stand out so startlingly. We see her for what she really is: a constant in our world with no ifs, ands, buts about it. She's always there and she's without pretense or makeup; she's a no-nonsense kind of girl. As early as shortly after noon, however, she puts on a few scarves and bonnets as clouds begin to build around some of her higher slopes. During summer afternoons, especially, we know a ruckus is brewing; momentum is feeding on itself, and we begin betting on whether there will be a good shower or merely a blow-over. Certainly, we put more eyes on the western rises than at any other time of day. We see her trying on one neckpiece after another, as if she is bargaining in a shop. About four o'clock, she decides to hurry out toward us (or so it seems) carrying a very wet deluge and enough wind to express her cargo to Kansas. Of course, Kansans may get only a wonderful breath of fresh air, and grumble about her stinginess.

Versatile, this octogenarian has many other performances up her sleeve. Some days she ingratiates herself into our moods for the sole purpose of soothing or, or conversely, heading us retrospectively down some forgotten and painful path. She throws around her shoulders robes and

Pikes Peak. Photo: Mary Andrews

cloaks of mist and fog. She yawns and says, "Don't wake me. I'm sleeping in today." We squint through curtains to see her faint outlines against the sky. As her contours come more sharply into focus, we aren't much interested in her foothills and the paths we've carved in her slopes. Trees are likewise not in our thoughts. She seems almost black in all the haze. Just the same, we know she's there, and if we keep squinting, her contours define themselves and restore our equilibrium.

When does she dazzle us the most? I'd say when she tries on different guises in late September, with her first snow. Oh, in warm sunny October she may strip down again to her summer shorts and sleeveless shirt, but she's flexing her muscles and considering her wardrobe for her next big spectacle, and the winter that lies ahead. Soon she'll bask in new white gowns, putting on one after the other, and strangely one on top of another. Doing only a little receding on sunny days, she'll stack on white coverlets again and again.

Her majesty proves she's a practiced performer, smiling and lounging until we, in our bundled-up world, just can't look any longer. Some of us want to leave her theater, go to Tucson. Depending on her whims, she may lambaste us at Christmas, give us a thin, clean, white blanket, or decide we really don't deserve pretty things. When spring pulls around, she may be so exasperated she throws on the only shawl she has left, drops her wetter-than-average deluge, taunting, "Get with it—haven't I given you enough, already? So, you are taking me for granted?" As her clouds plop down tubs of slushy mush in a final onslaught, we hear her "So, there!"

Of course, coquette that she is, she sometimes keeps her ermine in place until July, long after we've gone to her Alpine meadows to see delicate and colorful alpine flowers, plus all those hidden sparrows and chipmunks we haven't greeted for a whole year.

Well, she's really pretty nice. We don't appreciate her enough. Close your eyes and imagine her not there.

You can't! You feel guilty even thinking the thought.

"No, not wild parties! Wildlife -- Wildlife, the other kind." When I first came to my townhouse at Kentridge in 1991, I thought it had everything I needed except wildlife. That, I'd have to go elsewhere to find. But it wasn't long before I realized we had resident flocks of pigeons, crows, starlings, magpies - probably you could say we had resident house sparrows and house finches too. Not just right on our property, of course, but in the neighborhood. They came visiting. They called the vicinity home. And wasn't that a skunk I smelled? And mice in my garage? Of course, the squirrels liked running along the rails of my deck. Come August, there was a fresh, new garter snake by the front step.

By the time I ventured "up east" for walks near Sand Creek in late fall, I saw deer which had come in from bigger fields for some nibbling. Most memorable was the huge mule deer which took off to the north at an early hour and forded Platte Avenue. Your guess is as good as mine as to whether he missed all the on-coming vehicles at that hour.

It was several years before I realized the extent of the fox population (call it problem) in our area. When I did, it was because the folk living in the trailer court to the north of us fed them. Feeding is no longer happening on quite such a lavish scale (I think they learned they could be fined for littering, according to the Wildlife Department). They told me they fed because, if they did not, the foxes would come into their compound and kill their cats! They were right about one thing, the foxes are hungry and grow pretty thin by March.

My bird totals, however, are the ones which have grown tremendously since I've been at Kentridge, although at least a couple have ceased to be seen nearby. When I first came, there was a lovely flock of quail "up east." I saw these beautiful birds for only the first year. Meadowlarks likewise were on the property now occupied by a newly built church across the street. They no longer come so close, but there are a good many at a distance greeting the area with their unmistakable calls for much of the spring and early summer.

Over this thirteen-year period (and certainly counting every migratory season when many different birds come), species I have seen on the Kentridge property or nearby (or overhead) include, besides those already mentioned: grackle, starling, eastern blue jay, scrub jay, robin, flicker, mocking bird, lark bunting, western tanager, lark sparrow, sage sparrow, white-crowned sparrow, chipping sparrow, vesper sparrow, Bullocks oriole, orchard oriole, great blue heron, geese, mallards, and ring-billed gulls, the northern harrier, Cooper's hawk, sharp shinned hawk, Wilson's warbler, Virginia warbler, yellow-rumped warbler, American goldfinch, lesser goldfinch, bushtit, junco, towhee, Swainson's thrush, mocking bird, cedar waxwing, night hawk, downy woodpecker, Saye's phoebe, hummingbird, swallows of several kinds, shrike, brown thrasher, western kingbird, and killdeer.

Strangely, I never saw a chickadee on the property until very recently. The spring of 2000 proved fruitful with new warblers, the downy woodpecker, the lark bunting, and the lark sparrow. And in 2002, I saw the sage sparrow and the mocking bird. The orchard oriole was first seen in 2003.

Then there are all the creatures among us measuring less than four inches! "Up east" there are also many prairie wildflowers and numerous kinds of grasses. We don't really need wild parties at Kentridge -- watching wildlife is too much fun.

"Why all this courtship of nature?" Are we as blind when we woo her as we are when Cupid plays his devilish games? When we just can't get that certain other (in my case, Costa Rica) out of our minds, what's going on? And more significantly, is the affair going to engulf us in pain and humiliation, or bring out the best in us? When I can't come up with answers, I turn to the nature poets, Wordsworth, for instance . . . .

Way down the road where things get blurry, Costa Rica will still be vivid in my memory, but I wonder which of its images and adventures will be ones I'll always hark back to, ones like the time I

Howler Monkey in Costa Rica. Photo: Beth Ann Bassein

saw my first rose-breasted grosbeak in Weston, Missouri, or my first scissor-tailed flycatcher along a Texas road to Kerrville. Since a recent trip, scores of encounters in Costa Rica's wild act like they'll be tugging at me for a good long time and then come to some kind of permanent resting place in my consciousness. Will I ever forget river-rafting for the first time on a wild and delightful river or boating lagoons thirty-five miles back to an otherwise inaccessible lodge, where howler monkeys from imperceptible forest depths punctuate every dawn with their choruses? On the way there, we saw an anhinga, a jacana, a sloth, a crocodile, and scores of herons and egrets.

I surely won't forget the lavender water lilies we almost touched at the sides of our boat. Or, away from these damper regions, the wonderful deep orange flowers at the top of the erythrina trees, which shade coffee bushes. Then, one morning by the Siquirres River, there was the scarlet-rumped tanager in the tops of flowering trees that almost matched its momentary habitat. Something also sank in deeply about bathing in the hot waters from the Arenal volcano and twice hearing its stomach turn over in the agonies that produce so much rich soil on the high hillsides.

Nearby I saw a blue dacnis pair, blue and black birds the size of house finches. And the plate-sized butterfly that flew into the banana shed, just after we were told the US hires the cheapest help to trundle in eighty-pound stalks of a favorite fruit, will surely never float off my memory map. Tracking nature's diurnal journey hrough a hot afternoon on the Pacific shore dazed me into thinking I was headed for San Francisco, and when I turned around to go in the opposite direction, approaching Bogota. I was brought back to reality when evening unlocked racing hermit crabs at my feet and sparked a magnificent sunset -- Keats is right about Balboa discovering the Pacific from these shores.

Magpie Jay in Costa Rica.
Photo: Beth Ann Bassein

Dazzled -- is that the word? So enthralled we can't help remembering? Wordsworth knew about such memory: all his nature poetry, he said, was "emotion recollected in tranquillity." He was actually enthralled enough to say, "Nature never did betray the heart that loved her." Even if we are remembering the cyclone that littered the landscape (as Wordsworth likely was not), I doubt if we will stop having assignations with these dazzlers we cannot forget.

SPARKLING

There was nothing vague
about the deer I met this morning
in the middle of the trail
narrowed by scrub oak.
Feet firm to the earth,
body taut, she checked me out,
clicked one ear, leaped a green wall,
ran, every movement clean.
The towhee was as boldly defined:
cinnamon beret, white bib, black mustache,
tail olive like a spring aspen. Its ascent
to a perch was with flawless precision.
And the sky was pure, pure blue
with all clouds tied back over LA
or Liverpool. After this day,
night could not be other than crisp.

Sketch of Deer by Linda Wolfe.

18

III. FLORA

ART AND NATURE

Writers and other artists know that they have used nature as raw material for a long time. Wordsworth, as we've noted, talks about nature being a teacher. Thoreau saw good in the wild and free; he spent his life with nature and came away from it more comprehensive and comprehendible. Shakespeare, a derivative writer, may not have had time to examine the flower or the rock minutely, but he certainly talks about nature. Georgia O'Keeffe probably surpassed him in giving nature a close examination. She, like Conrad, wanted us, above all, to see.

Art necessitates an examination and then an effort to replicate, or, in some cases, exaggerate. Either approach quite probably begins by first seeing whatever is depicted "steadily and as a whole," as Matthew Arnold emphasized. If the artist's work is not like the original from nature, there is often the need for at least using nature as a take-off or starting point. If the art delves into the mysteries of the subconscious, the means by which it is rendered often are referenced through the realities of nature that canvas and paint, or other mediums, can render. Beyond the specifics gained from working with nature as illustrated in the art of Ikebana, for instance, there is also the effect this experience has on the practitioner of the art and the effect the flower arrangement has on the viewer. The art involved draws the flowers closer to both the practitioner and the viewer, causing those experiencing it to concentrate, examine, savor, admire, come to know.

Colorado Wildflowers.
Photo: Charles H. Smith

Many art forms begin by isolating an object -- an object of beauty, many would say, though beauty is in the eye of the beholder. Often the flower or weed or rock does not reveal its attraction until it has been isolated, seen by itself. The viewer, the learner, then works from a private set of inclinations and finds beauty or appreciation in an individual way through close inspection. Whatever our notions about beauty, we grow in the process of coming to understand, even if what we discover does not have a positive appeal.

We all know, of course, that an object may lose its lure when taken apart, that the symmetry and completeness of the whole flower, tree, or animal have a much greater effect than when broken down into parts. Although the opposite may sometimes be true, it is easy to see why Wordsworth said, "We murder to dissect." His statement needs to be qualified, of course, by the notion that we may lose more if we do not take the thing apart and look carefully at each component with all our senses in full play. Sight, smell, and touch help us get to the best and most complete understanding and reveal the natural object with all its compelling qualities.

Isolating the flower, pulling it away from its surroundings, and placing it on a blank canvas, allows us to exercise the notion that less is more. Chinese paintings have for centuries done this isolating for us. With nearly half of the canvas blank, our eyes move from rest to participation and we appreciate to a fuller extent in doing so. With less to explore, we concentrate more heavily on what remains. The Ikebana practitioner will tell you that while selecting, isolating, enhancing, and spending time with a flower, we come not only to understand it, but also to imbibe its beauty in such a way that we are enriched. Meditation on a flower is thus a process of coming to understand as well as appreciate. The experience moves through simplicity to understanding to gratification. There is nothing difficult about the process; in fact, it may seem all too simple.

Those learning about the natural world benefit from the talents of artists. Drawing is an enviable gift for the naturalist. In some instances, touching is taboo in dealing with nature. Smelling and tasting help considerably, but some parts of nature are out of reach. Much of nature exists soundlessly -- we cannot listen to flowers. Seeing is so important that it would be hard to call ourselves naturalists, if we did not use our eyes in the lab and in the field.

Watercolor of Columbines by Linda Wolfe.

Watercolor of Wild Iris by Linda Wolfe.

When asked about her flowers, Georgia O'Keeffe spoke explicitly about making us see. She said she wanted to focus our attention on the flower itself. She went through a period when she pretty much spurned frames, those with any attractiveness or width, because she did not want the viewer's attention to be drawn away from the flower. Pushing her flowers up in our faces, she wanted us to close out everything else. Such is the case with one of her works called "Iris." Bold colors, but no bolder than nature can produce, help push the long green stem and purplish, frilly globe toward us. Nothing recedes in Georgia's work. Viewers addicted to elaborate frames often ask why she put such an ugly one around "Iris," but she knew what she was doing. She did not want her audience to get lost in the superficial.

Georgia was not the first to help us look with intense concentration. Joseph Conrad speaks in like terms when he tells us a writer should, above all, make us see. Explicitness is the key. Putting stigma, style, and ovaries as well as beaks and butterflies where we can see them, even when they aren't nearby greatly enhances our knowledge, appreciation, and joy, as we capture the extremely varied world we live in.

Experiencing nature runs parallel to understanding ourselves. At least Wordsworth must have believed this to be true when he penned his lines about nature being a teacher. We come to see that we are far too prone to dismiss what is around us quickly, to fail to pause over it. Wordsworth would have us not only pause but later recollect what we have seen and put it into poetry. He must also have seen and experienced parallels between the human and the non-human. Seen in our entirety, we too are far more interesting than if we are broken down into parts and not completely understood. To quote Arnold again, understanding includes seeing a thing for what, "in itself, it really is."

One of the remarkable aspects of birdwatching and using binoculars is that, generally speaking, we do not interfere with nature. We do not dissect. Only occasionally do our observations make nature less. Our quick glance (maybe several) at the returning yellow warbler creates a specific, memorable moment that is implanted in us much as an artist hopes to implant an image that will grip and enlarge us, as it becomes a part of us. Capturing this image by camera or paint brush furnishes a secondary bonus which likewise enlarges us, in our private ways.

SECRETS OF SURVIVAL

When Gertrude Stein said, "A rose is a rose is a rose," she surely had something else in mind besides the absolute persistence of this flower. We know that 250 million years ago, there were a good many plants but few flowers, that they have not always been with us as they are now. And we know that the rose is and has been taking on different sizes, shapes, and colors during current memory, with help from scientists and horticulturists.

Gertrude would have been interested in the many ways in which flowers have evolved into extremely clever perpetuators of themselves. She would have marveled at their exploitation of insects, birds, and animals to carry pollen. She would have chortled with the rest of us at their use of color, odors, the comforts of a landing pad, chance winds, and traps to insure pollination.

Colorado Wildflowers.
Photo: Charles H. Smith

These adaptive measures make flowers unique and as interesting as animals and humans in their steadily evolving movement toward more than they have been.

When our prime viewing season for wild flowers is upon us, thinking about their reproductive life causes us to halt longer as we peer down at stamens and pistils, pause to take in odors, or experience the effusions of pleasure that brilliant blues, purples, reds, and yellows set in play. Flowers, of course, must give, in return for the help they get from pollinators outside themselves. Hummingbirds, like butterflies, bees, and bats, get all or part of their meals from flowers, as these animals and insects perform their pollinating service. Many flowers frequented by butterflies, such as Mexican sunflowers, bee balm, and verbena, even have a groove which guides the long tongue of the hummingbird or butterfly down to the nectar it craves. It is as if the flower created the V-necked dress with something other in mind than keeping cool.

Some flowers that bees frequent such as delphiniums have a lower petal at the front of the flower that functions as a handy place to land. Deeper inside, other flowers provide insects with a place to rest, hide from predators, and stay warm. Flowers even provide bees with a take-home package of glue they use to repair and seal their hives. While butterflies are attracted to bright colors, bats, with their poor eyesight, are drawn to the flowers with pronounced odors.

Some plants even signal to the pollinators that they are finished with pollination by changing their colors, as if they want to get on with the business of making seeds. The flowers of yucca close, and scents disappear. The blue bonnet has a white or yellow spot that lures bees to their favorite color. After the flower is pollinated, the spot turns red, a color bees can't see. "Don't bother now; it's all over," the flower seems to say.

Flowers with seemingly less purposeful mechanisms simply let the wind do their pollinating for them. They do not have to manufacture beautiful petals, pleasant perfumes, and sweet nectar. Pollination can occur just about any day because there is nearly always a breeze. One disadvantage to wind pollination is that these cautious flowers produce a wasted surplus of pollen, because they have less guarantee of how much pollen it will take to land some on a receptive female stigma.

Wind pollination works best in cold and temperate climates, while insect pollination works best in tropical climates where insects are more plentiful. Certain trees, shrubs, grasses, and seashore plants are particularly dependent on the wind for pollination. Although wind-pollinated plants do not have to develop elaborate sexual parts, such as we find in the iris or orchid, they do make the surface of their pollen feathery and their stigmas sticky in order to facilitate being easily carried and permanently lodged once they land. Wind-pollinated plants also improve their chances of pollination by producing tough little blossoms that last several days.

Not all flowers, however, are benevolent welfare outlets for the hungry. Some lure flies with a fetid smell, a handy place to lay eggs, or a warm shelter. The flower called Adam and Eve even contains starch which it burns primarily to produce heat. Once the flies have finished their chore of pollinating and partaken of all these conveniences, a good many of them remain in the blossom to be trapped and die. The jack-in-the-pulpit is another no-exit plant.

The next time you come upon a bed of wild flowers that you haven't expected to see, remember that chance may play a role in their being where they are. But the flower's making itself more presentable, so to lure in all the pollinators it can, may be just as pronounced. If you think beauty is not purposeful, think again. "A rose is a rose is a rose," greatly because it has slugged it out with extinction and been forced to make alterations along the way.

For more details on this subject, see the enjoyable book called *Sex in Your Garden* (1997) by Angela Overy, a Colorado gardener and writer associated with the Denver Botanical Garden.

THE PASQUEFLOWER AND THE MARIPOSA LILY,
ONE POISON, THE OTHER PALATABLE

Occasionally, as early as the last week of February, reports of seeing the first pasqueflower start filtering in. If the season is tricky enough, the last pasqueflower may be seen as late as mid-summer. This member of the buttercup family has other names: prairie anemone, windflower, blue tulip, American palstilla, and wild crocus. Cup-shaped, the pasqueflower's sepals are purple, violet or occasionally white. The blossom is one to one-and-one-half inches across and appears singly at the end of a stem which is two to sixteen inches tall. Several clusters appear on a branching root crown. The mainly basal and silky leaves are dissected by narrow linear divisions. As seeds ripen, the stiles grow, becoming long and feathery. After flowering, the stems continue growth.

Sketch of Pasqueflowers by Linda Wolfe

Field guides indicate that the pasqueflower begins blooming in early March at low elevations and is found through June at higher altitudes. The state flower of South Dakota, it appears at altitudes from 4000 to 9000 feet from Alaska south through Washington to Texas, and Illinois. Where I find it in Colorado, it is not abundant enough to have its volatile oil harvested for use in medicines. Its fine hairs and acridity make it a poor forage food. Domestic sheep founder on it.

Coming in view as late as July in Colorado, when numerous other wild flowers compete as conversation pieces, the mariposa lily or sego lily may surpass the pasqueflower in beauty and, in contrast, have a quite edible bulb. Called the star tulip or butterfly tulip, the mariposa has a single blossom that is triangular and cup-shaped. At Bear Creek Park, I search for single, but showy, specimens. Petals are yellowish white and marked with a crescent-shaped purple band or spot. Often growing on dry open plains and hillsides, it has a few grass-like leaves, a thin-coated bulb and, like most members of the lily family, three petals, three sepals and six stamens. Stems attain a height of eight to twenty inches.

Mariposa Lily.
Photo: Charles H. Smith

The mariposa is the only lily of the Rocky Mountain area that has white flowers and does not have three thin wings running the length of the seed pods. Its bulbous root, about the size of a walnut, is sweet, nutritious, and used for food by Native Americans, who sometimes grind it to make bread. The name *sego* is of Shoshonean origin. Generally referred to as the sego lily in Utah, it is this state's designated flower. During their first lean years in Utah, the Mormons consumed this bulb in large quantities, eating it raw or boiled like a potato. Bears, rodents, and sheep eat the bulbs avidly. Other members of the same genus contain starchy tubers that are also edible.

EVER PROLIFIC CACTI

The prickly pear cactus with its protective spines provides colorful flowers, water, and food in times when dryness prevents new growth and flowering in other plants. Each summer I see dozens of their pads, as their flat tongue-shaped, segmented stems are called, along the trails at Bear Creek Park. Fountain Creek Park has them also, where one of their popular names, the *plains cactus* is more apropos. The pads in June are on the verge of supporting flowers or establishing stability to do the same another year. Although their spines protect them from many marauders, a hail storm can blunt their profusion by breaking the lightly attached pads from their rooted base.

Ordinarily, however, they produce attractive flowers that are mostly yellow, though pink, rose, purple, and red specimens are found. Storing moisture, the pads furnish water for animals and sometimes humans when the need is dire. The thick leathery hide of the pads makes an excellent thermos for their somewhat bitter but potentially life-saving liquid.

Shape and spines give rise to two other popular names for the prickly pear, the *beaver's tail* and *devil's tongue*, but it is its fruit again that is responsible for another popular tag, the *Indian fig*. From their waxy flowers little knobs develop, ranging from the size of prunes to large lemons.

Prickly Pear Cactus.
Photo: Beth Ann Bassein

These fruits are sometimes yellowish green, purplish black, or red. Animals wanting them develop ways of brushing the spines aside; humans use protective leather gloves and blow torches for breaking off the spines, especially when harvesting them for cattle. Because they appeal to cattle, attempts have been made to develop a spineless variety. Doves, sapsuckers, and small desert animals harvest the seeds found in the dried fruits. Mountain sheep and deer feed on them, seeming not to mind the thorns.

For human consumption, the ends of the fruits are cut off and the pulp scooped out, or they can be peeled. The pulp is then made into candy or jelly; sometimes it is scrambled with eggs. Newer, more tender pads are quite edible when de-spined, sliced, boiled, or roasted. Some people like them cooked into a paste and fermented slightly. They can also be made into pickles. Dried seeds are ground into flour and used to thicken soups. Native Americans always dry and parch the seeds. The ruins at Mesa Verde reveal usage of this plant in 90 pecent of food remains examined. Grown over much of the US, they are more prevalent in the southwest, as well as in Mexico. The padres around California missions planted them for food and protection. In Mexico, it has still another name, *tuna*, and is sold from vegetable stalls; some US stores also currently stock it. Its Latin name, *opuntia macrohiza*, translates to *prickly pear on large roots or stalks*. Very similar to the *starvation cactus*, also aptly named from certain points-of-view, the prickly pear has more succulent fruits and less spiny pads. One prickly pear, that I sheepishly put in an outside pot and watched take root and grow, got several of its pads knocked off by hail. These lay flat in the flower pot and took root.

"AH, SUNFLOWER"—

William Blake (1757-1827) liked to watch sunflower stems bend and track the sun. Van Gogh's "The Sunflowers" (1888) sold for nearly forty million dollars in 1987. What this particular flower had to do with the price, I'd hesitate to say, but certainly around 1987, all our world began to fall in love with the sunflower's dark-brown centers surrounded by 20 or so brilliantly yellow petals. Still, we have stationery, neckties, cups, umbrellas, T-shirts, boxer shorts, door mats, calendars, barrettes, and bed sheets for sale that flash their big open faces. The Denver Botanical Garden also has a sunflower festival on its list of past celebrations.

Declared a decorative classic in the 1990's by the *Smithsonian*, they currently add variety and contrast to many bouquets prepared by florists. Although not quite as popular as a food for us as for birds, we welcome its seeds more than we ever have, among those choice sprinkle-overs at salad bars and as an ingredient in home-cooked specialties. In the world of high fashion, the sunflower's spunky image has caught on. Its appeal seems to come from its countenance, not its perfume.

Sunflowers.
Photo: Charles H. Smith

Tennessee seed caches dated around 3000 BC suggest the sunflower is native to the US. Native Americans used different parts of it to treat rattle snake bite, relieve chest pains, and heal cuts. The Hopis make a purple dye from the seeds. Others use sunflower oil for hair dressing. They also mix them in their breads. Made into a kind of granola bar, sunflower seeds were carried in packs when Native Americans made long overland trips.

Carried to Europe and now spread throughout the world, the sunflower found perhaps its most welcome acceptance in Russia, where by 1880 there were 400,000 acres of sunflowers under cultivation. Reportedly, a Russian can crack sunflower seeds on one side of the mouth, while dislodging kernels with the tongue and simultaneously spitting out empty hulls on the other side. Today nearly eighty-five percent of Russia's cooking oil comes from the sunflower. Undergoing a rise and fall in popularity during the last years of the 19th century, the sunflower's current rebirth for decorative and dietary uses is simply a repeat, a renaissance.

Growers of sunflowers face a number of challenges, even having to coax bears to let their fields alone. One farmer in Minnesota says bears lumber in, eat their fill and for fun, lie down and roll around, scratching themselves in the broken stalks. Trying to overcome the competition of mildew, wilt, rust, beetles, moths, midges, weevils, and black birds, scientists have worked to create sunflower hybrids and hazard-resistant varieties. And the big push is to develop a variety which can legitimately be labeled the lowest in saturated fat. Traditionally sunflower oil has less saturated fat than soybean, olive, and corn oils, but more than safflower and canola oils. About 300,000 tons of sunflower seeds are now sold annually for birds in the US.

Then there is the sheer joy of looking at a sunflower, or a whole field of them. Here is William Blake's early nineteenth-century response:

Ah Sun-flower! weary of time,
Who countest the steps of the Sun,
Seeking after that sweet golden clime
Where the traveler's journey is done;
Where the Youth pined away with desire,
And the pale Virgin shrouded in snow,
Arise from their graves and aspire,
Where my Sun-flower wishes to go.

RECIPROCITY—?

For many people yucca is not noticed for its cluster of useful gray-green bayonet-like leaves with a single thick central stalk covered with greenish-white to cream and purple tinged, drooping globular flowers. It is a plant they steer clear of, one that pricks, drawing blood. For some, even the flowers are not inviting because of the prickliness of the surrounding spikes or blade-like leaves. However we respond to this plant, the unique arrangement it has with the pronuba moth cannot help but intrigue.

Yucca.
Photo: El Paso County Parks Staff

Pausing, before we get close to a yucca plant of the Great Plains variety, we note the absolute symmetry of its clump of leaves and, if blooming, the absolutely perpendicular stalk of flowers. We may marvel at the plant's balance, as we do with many other flowers. Bending closely, we see that the leaves are alternate and radiate from the central stem with the newest blades appearing in the center, and in some cases growing to three feet in length and one to two inches in width at the base. In some varieties, the central stem sheds its leaves at the bottom producing a tall leafless trunk, the central cluster of leaves growing high like a dwarf tree. From the edges of these leaves, thread-like fibers strip and curl. Their surfaces are waxy and stiff; the tip end has a very sharp point.

The yucca many of us see in Colorado has large, oblong, upright fruits which are one or more inches wide and two to three inches long. Native Americans reportedly ate the young flowers in a salad, or as a potherb, and the fruits in a number of ways. One of the fifteen varieties found in the US, the datil yucca, furnishes a sweet, succulent fruit which can be eaten fresh or dried for later use.

Tasting somewhat like summer squash, though sweetly bitter, the fruit is harvested when fresh and young, both before and after it has developed seeds. Boiled down to a paste, it was made by Native Americans into a cake for drying. Yucca leaves contain salicylic acid and the roots saponin; eating them in quantities is not recommended.

Varieties differ as to when and how the fruits produce and disperse their seeds. The fruit in some types splits longitudinally into three sections, each holding when dry, the semi-round, flat, wafer-thin, winged seeds. Splitting the pod open, one can collect dozens of these black seeds from one plant. They have been pounded or ground into a meal for baking or strung as decorative beads.

Native Americans also used the fibers to make brooms, rope, baskets, leggings, mats, drapes, and sandals. Specimens of these can be seen wherever early Native American ancient artifacts are collected. The blades were soaked until soft and then pounded to get the fiber needed. Leaving the leaf fibers attached to the leaf tip, native peoples also devised a needle and thread for sewing. A soapy substance was extracted from the roots and used for washing hair. Yucca soap has been on the market minimally since 1900, and certain of the uses of it mentioned here can still be observed.

The largest of the yuccas is the Joshua tree; there are also at least two other varieties in the desert, the blue yucca and the Mojave yucca. The Great Plains yucca found in much of the West and East throughout the central states (here sometimes imported for decorative purposes) is called Spanish bayonet, bear grass, and soapweed. The word *yucca* is thought to derive from Native American usage.

One of the most intriguing aspects of the yucca involves the activities of the night-flying pronuba moth. Once inside the flower globe, the moth pricks the ovary and lays its eggs. It then collects from the anther the pollen which it stuffs into the funnel-shaped style. By making sure the pollen is at the bottom of the style, the moth assures pollination and ample food for its developing larva, which has been deposited there. Pollination will eventually result in producing hundreds of seeds so that both the yucca and the moth achieve posterity by the symbiotic process they are engaged in.

On the property where I grew up near Kansas City, Missouri, there were yucca plants between the front gate and the mail box. I always had the compulsion to jump a particular clump. Then, making a successful leap without being hooked on thorns was a rite of passage. No longer desperate for that kind of glory, I watch them with a different sort of interest.

Tumbleweed.
Photo: Beth Ann Bassein

If an exceptionally windy fall does not blow all the Colorado tumbleweeds to Kansas, March winds will do so. Maybe, however, you have an artistic neighbor who makes outdoor sculptures of them and tries to get them to hang around all year. Ian Frazier in *The Great Plains* reminds us that one of their main functions is poetic; the way they bounce and fly through the air, finally piling up against anything larger than they are, intrigues him. Anselm Hollo says they look like the skeleton of a brain.

Certainly folks on the plains come up with Americana like "The Tumbleweed Motel," "The Tumbleweed Cafe," and "Tumbleweed Liquors." In "The Tumbleweed Bar," the jukebox is liable to be playing "Tumbling Tumbleweeds," a favorite western song by the Sons of the Pioneers. "Tumbleweeds" has been a favorite syndicated cartoon strip. They blow before a Kansas tornado at the beginning of "The Wizard of Oz" and are a signature for dozens of western films: a tumbleweed rolls across a deserted street or a vast prairie, the hero charges in on a horse with more mettle than most could possibly possess, and the bad guy feels to see if his pistol is still where he put it. Price Strowbridge, a poetic mailman on the plains, compared them to a herd of buffalo as they charged over the countryside. Their elusive passing makes us wonder about source point and destination.

Quite probably some of Colorado's tumbleweeds, certainly those first found in Nebraska and the Dakotas, came from Russia, which has, in its seven hundred mile wide belt of prairie, stretching eastward from Hungary for 3,500 miles, a favorable locale for them. This area is colder than our southern plains and drier than our northern plains, windy, and empty. In the 1870's thousands of German Catholics, Mennonites, Huberites, Amish, and others left southern Russia for the Great Plains. Many of these were peoples who had been adrift in Europe since the Protestant Reformation 350 years before. They brought their bushel of Crimean wheat with them for planting, and, of course, it contained seeds of the Russian thistle tumbleweed.

Some of the most thriving invasive plants of the Great Plains are not native and like the tumbleweed came from abroad with early settlers. Before settled by homesteaders, the Great Plains had no Russian knapweed, no goat grass, no cow cockle, no summer cypress. Corn cockle, which grows with winter wheat and makes bread taste strange when it gets ground into the flour, came from Russia. Cheatgrass, which is not eaten by cows but takes over pastures, also came from Russia. Many of these plants do some tumbling.

The Russian thistle tumbleweed is found in North Dakota and Nebraska, particularly the western part. Another tumbling plant, a native to the US found on our dry prairies, is the tumble pigweed. Found in cultivated and fallow fields, on roadsides, and in waste places, this plant has narrower leaf blades than the prostrate pigweed.

Both the Russian and native varieties flower from August to October. The flower and seed of the Russian variety are larger than the pigweed and grow taller. The pigweed variety forms a more globe-shaped plant. The stems of the Russian tumbleweed are usually red streaked and more prickly than the native plant.

The Russian thistle, also called Russian cactus, saltwort, prickly glasswort, and weed witch by us, is called *perekati-pole* by the Russians, meaning *roll across the field*. Seedlings of both tumbleweeds can be found in dry, sandy soil in the spring. For two months, the green plants are edible by livestock. When the weather is warmer, they get hard, woody, and prickly, crowding out other plants. In the early fall, the stalk breaks loose from the ground. A single plant may have from 10,000 to 100,000 seeds, which fall off as the wind takes them hither and yon. Traveling many miles, the seeds stay vital for years. Of all plants that come loose from their moorings, the Russian thistle tumbleweed is the best traveler and the hardest to control. They do roam like a buffalo.

Native Americans harvested the seeds from tumble pigweed and ground them into flour. Hay made from the Russian thistle tumbleweed was an important survival food for cattle during the drought of the 1930's. Small animals and song birds consume the seeds, and tumbleweeds make excellent cover for pheasants. Russian thistle and pigweed tumbleweeds can contain dangerous levels of nitrates and may be harmful to livestock.

INVESTIGATING A TREE

The oak tree back of my childhood house
shutting off my view
was formidable and impervious.
I never dared look behind it.
I could learn about wilderness elsewhere.

We had only this one oak, the rest
were maple, walnut, hickory.
My brothers implored this oak to shed acorns.
That was after summer
when meaning took over.

We never watched a tenacious snake
fall from this oak's branches,
as it wrestled with grackles attacking en masse.
Nor were wrens prone
to solo from its limbs.

Rooted to a slope not good for walking,
our oak had secrets all right,
and I feared what it withheld.
I cowered while it stood symmetrical
and kept me from cavorting before it
in my flimsy nightgown.

Partha among the leaves.
Photo: Katherine Bassein/Rajarshi Roy

IV. FAUNA: THE CRITTERS

THE LITTLE BIG TOP

We mostly know fleas as little black specks not more than a few times as large as the period at the end of this sentence. We need an extra nudge to our naturalist bent to get interested in these wingless insects which live on birds, mammals, and us, if we get near them, or they us. Like house sparrows, termites, mice, and perhaps several other insects, they can be victims of fly swatters and poison, in just about any house on the block. Only the sparrow has any legal recourse. Formidable, however, the fleas are, for North America has 250 of the near 16,000 species world wide.

Fleas have laterally flattened abdomens with many protruding spines and bristles, which do not stop them from easily slipping between the feathers or hairs of their hosts. Tough skinned, they are difficult to crush. They can make spectacular leaps, some as high as eight inches and as far as thirteen. They have minute, compound eyes, or none at all. Their mouth parts have three piercing stylets for sucking blood. Often they lay their eggs in their host's nest and sometimes attach eggs directly to the host's hair or feathers. The larvae pupates in silk cocoons, but many remain dormant for long periods until stimulated by vibrations indicating the approach of a host. Rumor has it that they know to frequent areas which are the hardest to scratch.

The family *pulicidae* contains most of the fleas that attack people and domestic animals. Many are named after their principal host; hence, there are cat fleas, human fleas, and rat fleas. Fleas on rats infected by bubonic plague spread the disease throughout Europe during the Middle Ages. This fact alone reduces the flea so completely that its elevation to popular appeal becomes the challenge of all challenges. How better to achieve this coveted goal than to put them into show business! Displaying them taxes belief and teases the funny bone, while it caps the list of curiosities.

Stories go that one Bertolotto had a little big top circus which featured four elegantly dressed fleas doing a waltz and a twelve-piece flea orchestra performing on small instruments. A flea fantasia, it was called. After his show, Bertolotto rolled up his sleeve and let his performers feast on his arm. He also invited the audience to feed the fleas in like manner. This entertainment came to the US with P. T. Barnum's Flea Circus, appearing on Broadway in 1842. Roy Heckler's similar show, begun much later, lasted until the 1950's and featured a flea chariot race, a flea merry-go-round, and dancing fleas in hoop skirts. Seemingly reliable sources say especially trained fleas have been flown to Hollywood to perform in the movies. Adam Gertsacov, whose Acme Miniature Circus is based in Providence, Rhode Island, believes this lost art can be revived.

We need to remember that the flea circus got its start in an era when we scratched more than we do now. The era was one in which the lap dog gained popularity, because it was believed that by holding the little dog on one's lap, the fleas would leave the human body alone and move to the dog's. No mercy for the dog!

"WITCH DOCTORS AND MULE KILLERS"

Called aggressive predators, amazing fliers, and strange suitors, dragonflies have redeeming beauty to offset a not-so-savory reputation. Folklore has it that they are servants of snakes, sometimes reviving them. They are also Lazarus-like causing creatures to rise from the dead. Besides being snake doctors, they are the devil's darning needle, because they can sew wicked children's lips shut while they sleep. When not doing this cruel kind of handiwork, they are mule killers. Around for two hundred million years and part of a species group of five hundred, they have had time to promote more than their share of lore.

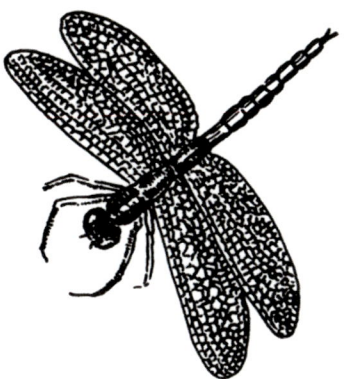

Dragonflies eat as many as three hundred mosquitoes a day. In some localities old bathtubs are planted to catch water so there will be favorable, but limited, breeding areas for mosquitos and their enemy, dragonflies. They do not damage crops. Often confused or compared to damselflies, they can be differentiated by noting that dragonflies are larger and fly like helicopters, while damselflies flutter like butterflies. Dragonflies also spread their wings out to the sides, while damselflies tend to fold theirs over their abdomens. Dragonflies have wrap-around incandescent red eyes, which meet in many species at the back of their heads, making a field of vision of 360 degrees.

Sketch of Dragonfly by Linda Wolfe

They also spend most of their lives under water. Both dragonflies and damselflies have a lip one third the length of their bodies folded underneath their heads, making it look like a beard. The dragonfly is one of the fastest insects clocked and can lift double its own weight. They perform all the antics of a stunt pilot including stopping in mid-air, reversing, hovering, and somersaulting. Their wings are exceedingly strong, well braced, and capable of bending. A dragonfly does not necessarily beat all its wings at once but can beat one or more to perform acrobatic maneuvers. They are equipped to cooperate with the airflow, adjusting as its changes occur. Their eyes permit them to spot prey at a distance of one hundred feet.

Much easier to study than birds because they can be netted with less equipment, dragonflies are aerialists that have taken advantage of every improvement evolution has lent them to arrive at highly advanced operational techniques. To follow their maneuvers is to be on the cutting edge of animal strategy.

FROGS

play pattycake on the inside wall
of their mama's stomach
get slurped into papa's tuba, spat
out in due time, herded
onto papa's back
dropped to be mothered by desert,
frozen pools, rushing streams,
the depths of a termite mound.

*Frog Photo: El Paso
County Parks Staff*

Young as the last rain
they chirp and whir into wedlock.
Some stick to rocks with suction cups
some have built-in antifreeze
others store water under their skin.
Tree frog, torrent frog, laced-lid frog, bull frog
all old as dinosaurs
expendable but dependable
until caught in a scalding chemical
where eyes appear on shoulders
legs are cut off at the knee,
arms fracture to feet
which plead like hands, prayerfully
in desert, pond, creek.

If you want to explain relativity, diversity, and ambiguity, look to an often overlooked creature in our locality -- the termite. It is small, yet it can occupy a space as large as a football field; it is a destroyer, yet very useful as a preserver; it is secretive, yet overwhelmingly bold one night of the year; it inspires lyrics and stories as well as dread and superstition; it seems a simple critter, yet it lives in a highly structured society.

Measuring as little as a third of an inch and weighing less than a thousandth of an ounce, termites make their presence felt through quantity. Experts estimate there are a thousand pounds of termites on earth for every human. When termites raid the night once a year in search of mates, as many as 15,000 can be caught in an average household bucket. There are 2,300 known species.

Anyone interested in architectural preservation had better know about termites. These fluttering insects with dull, diaphanous wings eat entire homes! But from a relative point of view, they are also extremely useful recyclers. Richard Conniff, author of *Spineless Wonders,* tells us that if they were not out breaking down fallen and dying trees and plants, and returning nutrition to the land, new trees would not live. Additionally, neither would we.

Termites hate open air, except on the night when they are crazed into finding a mate. Subtle, they build tubes up the house foundation to move back and forth between food and nest. Many species are thus sealed off from the outside world doing their destructive work from within. They intermitently open kickout holes to dump out their fecal pellets. Most homeowners don't recognize this grit on their floors; if they do, they may have slipped head over heels on it.

Persons more knowledgeable about termites will hear their faint clicking -- are they smacking their lips? Europeans believed this sound was a harbinger of death invading their houses. Some believe this superstition gave termites their name: the Greek word *terma* means the end. On the lighter side, children's books have been written about Teddy and his sly ways. Such levity relieves despair, of course, when the legs of a grand piano suddenly collapse or plunge through a "rotten" floor.

Termites have an elaborate social structure whereby a few do the reproducing, and the rest serve their associates by tending the young, bringing food, building nests, or fighting intruders. Most termites give up the chance to reproduce, letting the King and Queen deliver the *alates*, which fly forth on one romantic (and often fatal) night of the year. The King and Queen are devoted to one another, remain together fifteen to twenty years, and produce up to 30,000 eggs a day.

Some are soldiers only: they go so far as to swell their abdomens until they explode, splattering guts all over the enemy. Foraging, regurgitating, and grooming are other tasks assigned to those who don't reproduce. Adaptive, they may feed the young from both ends of their digestive track. "Chemical messages" from the Queen passed to offspring prompt them to become soldiers and socially minded assistants of several kinds.

Becoming prodigious engineers, they build elaborate structures including spiral staircases and umbrellas; they use a north-south orientation and establish extensive underground auditoriums at a distance from mounds. Recent studies show that these mounds are built with elaborate ventilation. What amounts to vast assembly plants then offer Teddy and all his cousins and friends space for their work. They even enlist fungi to make their food more digestible. Where there has been a termite mound, trees readily grow.

VOLES—NOW YOU SEE ONE, NOW YOU DON'T

At intervals, a dead vole appears out of nowhere along the trails at Fountain Creek Park. When we read that there are at least a dozen different voles of the *microtus* species that may inhabit the same territory, one we could easily traverse, our interest is piqued. When we learn one researcher found that with 100 pairs of voles living on forty acres of land, their offspring reach a total density of 8,900 between April and September, we start thinking in terms of a mass influx, an irruption. The number seen at any given time would belie this notion. One reason we don't see many of them is that they run in open areas and only slow down when they reach shelter. Living both a terrestrial and subterranean life, they don't move into houses at the rate mice do.

Voles have a stocky body, a blunt nose, and small ears only a little longer than their body fur. The meadow vole is from three and one-half to five inches long with a tail one and two-fifths to two and three-fifths inches long. Their coarse fur is brown or gray. Their incisors are open rooted and always growing, the better to mow down and crunch the plants they feed on. The female has eight mammary glands. When born, her young have no external hair, are pink with closed eyes and ears. Hair begins to appear by day five. Wandering begins at two weeks and weaning at three weeks. Mature voles make a high squeaky sound, but newborns have a soft breathless chirping that increases in vigor as they grow. The vole's senses are highly developed, especially touch. Their vision is good for short distances, and they respond readily to sounds and odors.

A very high rate of reproduction insures continuation of the vole's numerous species. Females may become pregnant at three weeks. Males require six to eight weeks to produce mature sperm. This discrepancy between the sexes is thought to prevent inbreeding because the young males are not able to impregnate until they have scattered from the parental nest. A short gestation period of twenty to twenty-three days also helps to produce a high level of reproduction.

Voles construct well-kept runways on the surface of the ground, but all species burrow to some degree to make their nests, which are used as nurseries, resting areas, and for protection. Nests are made of dried grass and plant fibers; they can be placed under rocks or logs, boards, fence posts, hay bales, and brush piles. Voles are hampered by not being able to travel far for food; hence they take advantage of root vegetables, beans, melons, hay. Quick to adapt to the food available, they are considered a pest.

Researcher Richard Ostfeld states that voles manage their habitats by keeping woody plants from invading the grassy fields they prefer. They also play a role in preserving areas favored by deer, turkeys, and bluebirds. Hawks and owls especially make use of the vole for food. Perhaps the dead ones I've seen in Fountain Creek Park have been dropped from the beak or claws of these eager, winged aggressors. Northern shrikes, magpies, ravens, great blue herons, and bitterns also lunch on them as do badgers, coyotes, foxes, skunks, weasels, wild cats, snakes, trout, and salamanders. The vole, in turn, may munch on our garden vegetables and in plots where tender nursery stock is grown. Their diet is so varied, however, they may lead healthy lives far from these precious plants.

COYOTES ACLAMORING

Sketch of Coyote and Vole
by Linda Wolfe

The gathering of coyotes leaves
no space for the likes of me,
unless they know I am listening.
That would pull them in, to go at it
more quietly. I imagine their congress
has to do with sealing territory,
celebrating a treaty about to be instilled.

That their yelps vary along the scale
from the young piping up with immediate plans
to the oldsters spending long hours to thump
out a long-range proposal, I've no doubt.
Alone, I am glad for their clamor, glad
for any message that distance
is not a vacuum waiting to be filled.

V. FAUNA: THE FLYERS

WHY THE BIRD --

Who can say how the Cooper's hawk
perched outside my window regards me
as I sit beside a lit candle in my living room
where days are distinguished by drawing the blinds,
opening the blinds, searching the skies for clouds?
Likely, it doesn't see me as a part of the room
but as a force so threatening I am extracted from it.

Cooper's Hawk
Photo: El Paso
County Parks Staff

I want to be more than a threat in a house
on a street that runs beside other streets
and peters out at the edge of the prairie,
a prairie that stretches all the way to Kansas.
After that, forms a continent. Then joins other
continents and flickers in a far-off galaxy.
The hawk sets off on wings that flap and float
as it searches local pastures and hillsides.

In my candle flame I search for a magic
that sensitizes my remoteness, cancels my lethargy,
under a sky where clouds bring no electrical outages,
just spring rain, a place where I am more than a woman
in a house on a street that peters out at the edge
of the prairie. Ah, but better than magic is the hawk:
once it perches before me, I forget everything
except its piercing eye. When I catch
the glint of this eye, I sense the power of wings.
When this bird bursts into motion, I too am flying.

Roger Tory Peterson tells us the white-throated sparrow's song is made up of several clear pensive whistles, then some clear notes followed by three quavering notes in a different pitch. To really know this song, it takes an early spring morning when the world seems hollowed out just for you, and the "pensive whistles" permeate something deeper than common sounds can reach. The "clear notes" allow you to hold the haunting whistle while you wish it would happen again. And it does. A little elf from a magic kingdom has come to entertain you.

We know a good many things about bird songs, but much comes to us in snatches and reports of individual cases, which may not have been tested sufficiently to establish patterns. Recordings, sonograms or spectro-graphs, computer programs, and collections like those in the Cornell Library of Natural Sounds are, however, creating a "golden age of birdsong study," according to Don Stap, writing in the March, 1999, issue of *Audubon Magazine*. We know that bird songs are directly related to mating and asserting the right to territory. Nowhere in my readings do I find anyone disputing this dual claim, or that communication between the young and its parents and maintaining the composition of a flock are not also reasons for their pealing forth wherever we find them.

Deceiving might also seem to be a factor in some singing, at least in the imitative songs of the mocking bird or the starling, but how can anyone be sure? I was told by one person that birds sing to help their digestion; this notion was uttered, I believe, to deflate all those who think birds sing because they and we appreciate the beautiful. There is something in us that wants to put down such mundane reasons for their singing.

Beyond the basics, there are various areas of study where startling information has been brought forth, but which leave explanation more open. Seemingly like children, white-crowned sparrows must hear parents sing in order to sing like them. If they hear song sparrows sing, they will sing like song sparrows. Some birds do not cease to sing when courtship is over; the common yellowthroat sings during every stage of nesting, except courtship. The American redstart sings throughout courtship and mating until the nest is built; then it sings another song. What drives the change? Are we talking about work songs or love songs? Female cardinals, Baltimore orioles, and rose-breasted grosbeaks sing as do males in many species. Are there other females which sing? There has not been much research on the female bird singing. Does she hum along with the best of the males, or just consider herself lucky not to have to learn all those tunes?

Some birds sing differently at different times of the day. Chipping sparrows have one basic song, while brown thrashers may have as many as 2000 (one source says 3000) song types. The eastern meadowlark and the western meadowlark have very different songs. Some birds are said to have regional dialects; these dialects alter if the bird moves to a different territory where its own species has a different dialect. Some birds learn their songs during the first seven weeks, while others take much longer. Some do counter-singing by matching others in song. They may move into a variation which is matched or countered by the other participant in the duo. Wrens are especially prone to join in this game. One area currently receiving more concentration is the recording of more than one species at once, in order to understand better the relationships between one species and another.

The vocal organ of birds is the syrinx, which is at the lower end of the trachea and surrounded by an air sac, all of which is deep in the breast cavity. The syrinx becomes a resonating chamber and vibrates in conjunction with very elastic membranes. Sets of muscles control the movement of the syrinx. The membranes can be adjusted like the skin of a drum. Birds vary both the loudness and frequency of sounds by altering the air pressure passing from the lungs to the syrinx, and by varying the tension of syringeal muscles. Biologists say the two sides of the syrinx are independently controlled so that some birds develop a two-voiced repertoire.

What a wonderful instrument the bird's syrinx is! Comparable to the special equipment of the opera singer -- ? We watch all singers, human or avian, and think they possess a marvelous built-in flute. The pleasure they bring is ours whether the performer is a white-throated sparrow or a diva.

Or elf!

CLEANLINESS IS BIRDLINESS

Having just undergone the trauma of a major paint job and floor replacement, I'm super charged with an obviously futile desire to keep my quarters clean. Noticing that many used bird nests don't look as if a birdlet ever squirted a berry in the wrong direction or upchucked a caterpillar, I wonder how they keep their domiciles so neat. Those examining the waste management strategies of birds point to their special equipment and their cleaning efforts, sometimes on an hourly basis.

Birds differ a good deal from fish and mammals in managing their protein intake. Protein contains many amino acids, and each of these contains a nitrogen group. This nitrogen is used in a variety of ways by the body but must eventually be excreted. Fish excrete the nitrogen as amonia into the water around them which is then diluted so it does not harm other living organisms. Mammals change the nitrogen to urea, which is not as harmful as amonia; it is stored in their bladders and passed as the urge rises. The accumulation of urine, however, increases the animal's body weight and causes it to want to drink often. Neither of these effects are in the best interests of birds: they do not wish to waste time looking for water, and it is not desirable that they have the increased body weight that a bladder would add.

Birds are thus conveniently equipped with the means of avoiding the toxic amonia that fish excrete, and they have no urinary bladder. Birds metabolize nitrogen waste to uric acid that is a white, chalky, and non-toxic substance. They also possess a cloaca which is a compartment at the end of their large intestine that opens directly to the outside by way of a vent, or anal opening. The cloaca receives egested waste from their intestines. Quick to dry, the bird's excretions more quickly disintegrate and often seem to vanish.

Although young birds usually defecate after each feeding, the cells lining their cloaca secrete a gelatinous material that surrounds the waste and forms a soft capsule. After eating, the young birds eject these neatly packaged fecal sacs. The adult bird waits for these sacs to be dropped, grabs them in its bill, takes them a distance from the nest, drops them, or eats them. Hence, we never see great accumulations of wastes in many of those bird nests that blow from trees or otherwise get into our possession from time to time, or that we peek into. In addition, the bird's method of disposing of these wastes helps decrease diseases, parasites, and odors that might attract predators.

Birds do not need mops and vacuum cleaners, or new floors and paint jobs. Just a little repair each spring, and maybe the rinse of a nice rain.

Roger Tory Peterson lists bushtits as year-round residents along the California coast and inland in Oregon, Nevada, Utah, Arizona, New Mexico, Colorado, and southward into Mexico. Probably because of the greater visibility of all birds during leafless winter, I tend to see them more often in the cool or cold months than in spring and summer. They are relatively quiet birds, and if they didn't move in flocks, I might mistake them for other small gray birds. They don't

Bushtit
Photo: Donald Waite/Cornell

make too much noise, but their conversations in groups consist of tsits, lisps, and clenks, as they move from ground to bushes to trees. During courtship time, they produce calls and trills.

They have been known to move in flocks of 70, but smaller flocks are more common, where they are sometimes in the company of chickadees, warblers, titmice, wrens, and kinglets. They roost close together to utilize and conserve heat. The bushtits I have seen at the Pueblo reservoir and at Bear Creek and Fountain Creek parks have mostly been adorning drabber bushes, but one flock at Fountain Creek, not far from the nature center, was at the edges of the irrigation ditch on a sandy and partially snow-covered area. Measuring only 4 inches, part of their lure is their smallness.

The bushtit's nest is a gourd-shaped hanging basket woven and supported by twigs. Moss, lichen, leaves, cocoons, grass, and flowers are fastened into this nest with spider web. The pocket is lined with plant down, hair, and feathers. Eggs are white. They eat insects including spiders and feed their young solid foods. Ehrlich, Dobbin, and Wheye say if they are disturbed during nest building, egg laying, or incubation, they desert the process, select new mates, and begin again. Male and female roost in the completed nest. Both sexes take part in raising the young by foraging for their supply of food.

Actually they have more color than we first assume. They have pale underparts and brownish cheeks. Males of those found in southwest New Mexico and west Texas have black or black-flecked cheeks. The iris of the eye is pale cream in adult females and dark brown in juveniles and adult males. Stubby bills and longish tails also help identify them. Admittedly, they may not be as striking as the chickadee with its black, white, and gray markings. They lack the titmouse's crest, and many juncos have a greater variety of hues. Nuthatches have their characteristic movements and one variety has a red breast.

The bushtit's sense of community seems to be its most striking feature. Does their smallness create greater need for companionship?

THE HERMIT THRUSH

The hermit thrush seen at Fountain Creek Regional Park in mid-February made its presence felt much before the one Walt Whitman said came out of hiding and pealed forth its flute-like music during the days after April 14, 1865. Those were the days when Abraham Lincoln's hearse was rolling slowly by train from Washington, DC, where he had been shot, to Springfield, Illinois, and when people came out at every town to bow in respect.

Hermit Thrush. Photo: J.R. Woodward/Cornell

Whitman loved to walk along the shore and doubtlessly other places; he was not a novice at identifying birds. Still, he may have been engaging, to some extent, in hyperbole as he wrote his very beautiful elegy to Lincoln, the "fallen hero." Knowing the reclusiveness of the hermit thrush, he may have chosen it for that very reason -- here was a bird making the supreme sacrifice to come out of hiding and "sing by himself a song," because the nobility of Lincoln demanded it. Of course, we know singing picks up in spring. Having this bird sing in April, as Whitman witnessed it, would be appropriate and quite usual.

Ordinarily a bird of the forest floor, the hermit thrush may have given up for the occasion its habit of cocking its tail, then lowering it slowly. Did it also throw its head high over its olive green back to give its voice full range and allow its spotted breast to glitter in the sun? Whitman, at any rate, worked his imagination into these possibilities.

Henry David Thoreau, another walker, made no distinction between the hermit thrush and the wood thrush. Writing a little earlier than Whitman (and about what is now believed was the hermit thrush, not the wood thrush), he says the "fine metallic ring" in the bird's song expresses the immortal beauty and wildness of the woods. He wants to go in search of the bird but discovers it may be ventriloquizing because it seems further off than it truly is.

Thoreau's further thoughts may be closer to those of Whitman's than first realized. Just as the church through which Lincoln was drawn back to his former home was America's natural scene, Thoreau says of the music the thrush creates: "He makes a Sabbath out of a week day. I could go to hear him, could buy a pew in his church."

Of the dozen or so thrushes found in many bird guides, including the different robins and bluebirds, the Townsend's solitaire, the veery, and the wheatear, perhaps the four that we puzzle most over are the Swainson's, the hermit, the wood, and the veery. All four of these can at first be mistaken one for the other. The Swainson's has a conspicuous buffy eye-ring, buff on its cheeks and upper breast. The wood thrush is rusty headed, smaller than a robin, plumper than the other brown thrushes, has a deepening rufous about the head plus striped cheeks, and rounder, more numerous breast spots. The veery is uniformly brown above and gray on its flanks. It does not have a strong eye-ring. It is the least spotted thrush. The ones found in the West are darker brown than those in the East. All of their songs are different, although the song of all of them has been described as flute-like.

It is not impossible to see several of the thrushes in residential areas, especially in the spring, where tree branches are close to the earth, and when it has recently rained. Peterson tells us that the veery and the Swainson's winter south of the US, but that the hermit thrush may winter in the US. The wood thrush breeds more in the eastern US, and the veery mostly north of Colorado, while the hermit and the Swainson's are more likely to be seen in our area in summer. None are, however, plentiful like the American robin or so used to humans. The hermit thrush, rightly named, is not very curious about us.

THE PHILOSOPHER'S CAVE

More times than not when I am at the desk at the Fountain Creek Nature Center, I see a belted kingfisher sitting on a branch over the edge of the pond. Because this bird always seems in deep thought, I would, if I had a pet kingfisher, call it Socrates or Hypatia. Both of these philosophers sat thinking, long and hard. Both surely had wild hair and looked purposely ahead trying to better themselves. Being philosophers, they naturally were solitary, hours on end. Obviously the kingfisher's stubby legs are not meant for long-distance running. Its wings help when moving into lofty pursuits. When I see a kingfisher, I am Plato coming for a tete-a-tete with some great philosopher of Athens.

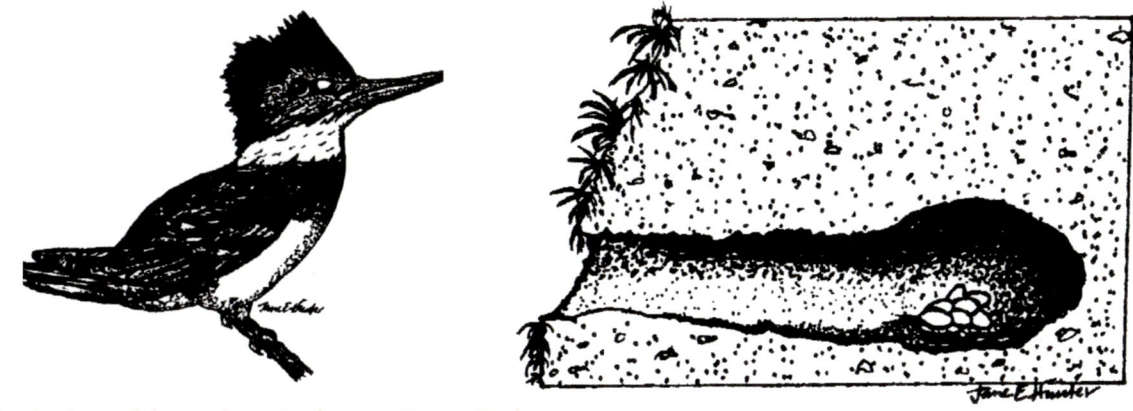

Sketch of Kingfisher and its Nest by Jane Hunter Zook

Along with intense powers of concentration, the kingfisher nonetheless points its beak as if it were an arrow about to connect. Its eyes focus down this stiletto with a pressure that makes its head feathers rise. Helped to focus by its white eye spot, nothing is missed. Except for their breeding and nurturing season of about seven weeks, both the male and female are solitary, claiming separate fishing territories and defending them.

Measuring up to thirteen inches, our belted kingfishers live near water, because their diet is primarily fish. With the wisdom of the ages, kingfishers pound the fish against their perch to stop its flopping and to position it so it will go down head first. Their capacity to get by on snakes, insects, and birds, if fish are not available, and their relatively few competitors make for maximum survival, even with only one brood per year. Although the US has only the belted kingfisher, and in south Texas the green kingfisher, there are around 80 species worldwide. In Kenya, some are very small and brightly luminous, while others are very large and black and white pied.

Unique among birds, our belted kingfisher female, with her rufous belly, is the one of the pair most brightly colored. Strikingly different also is her nesting site. Digging a cave in a vegetable-free dirt bank, partners begin by burrowing about a foot and a half below the top of their chosen mound. Their entrance is about three inches in diameter and takes them down a three-to ten-foot tunnel which widens into a circular nesting area at the end. A clever choice for a nesting area, this cave affords greater protection and chances of survival. I'd say, philosophically speaking, they have chosen a splendid place to shut out all the distractions of the world and get into the nitty-gritty of what makes the world tick.

As part of their nurturing period, the young birds are taught to dive for objects in ponds and lakes. Wise, the parents give lessons by throwing in dead matter so the young can practice retrieving it. I have never seen them reading scholarly texts, but perhaps there are more ways than one to channel lofty mental pursuits.

THE WHITE PELICAN

sleeps at night on one of the small islands,

White Pelican
Photo: El Paso County
Parks Staff

sleeps until the sun warms the water.
The early ducks preen while it tucks
its bill and eyes under feathers, seems oblivious
to quacking and other web-footed behaviors.
Whole flocks fly low over the pelican's head,
going no place in particular, just taking off
at the approach of a man with a camera,
just landing to do what ducks do before noon:
turn their bottoms up to beak inverts from below,
walk the shore for nibbles of sand.
When the white pelican finally slides off
the island, one mallard pumps a wing,
but, like the pelican, never alters
instinct enough to sing.

44

Intrigued by Ron Noel's report that a pine siskin sat on his finger, I decided to check what the experts say about familiarity between this bird and humans. I wanted to know if my friend Ron has special charms or if he met an extra friendly siskin. I found only one writer saying that siskins are sometimes tame as they feed on nearby seedpods or at feeders. But that was enough to make me more envious of my friend's experience and give me hope of being on some siskin's partiality list.

For those of you who have relegated the pine siskin to the little brown bird category, some distinguishing features are in order. Watch them fly, and you will see yellow in their wings and on the underside of their deeply notched tails. Their bills are thin and pointed and will keep you from mistaking them for female house finches. Male and female siskins are similarly colored.

Pine siskins like cone-bearing forests but can be found in mixed woods, weedy areas, parks, and suburbs. Nesting often occurs where there are pines with heavily needled branches. Nests will be near the ends of these branches, where needles are more pronounced and concealing. They are year-round residents of Colorado, nesting more in the western half of the state.

Semi-colonial, they may build nests only a few feet apart. When foraging in flocks, they tend to move down from the top of a tree in a compact group, then move in a circular flight to another tree, where they repeat their effort. Winter flocks usually have from fifty to two hundred birds, but they have been seen in flocks as large as one thousand. Nomadic, they also fly in mixed flocks with goldfinches, a bird sharing the same genus, with juncos, and with crossbills. They may migrate altitudinally.

Their diet includes seeds, forbs, floral buds, and sap. Males are attentive providers of food for their family through courtship and through the period before the young fly. They are small, measuring only five inches in length but have a considerable wing span of nine inches. Quick, they keep up with the juncos and finches as they glean.

Find pine siskins with other little birds at your feeders and on the ground under them. Tell me if one sits on your finger.

FORCED EVACUATION

Smoke cloaks the mountain.

I sniff the heavy air, envision heat

driving pine siskins from high meadows

to lowland gardens.

I fashion their escape

from burning aspen groves,

their wings making a softer sound

than the crackling fire near them.

I pause while they

finish small harvests

before piloting their weight

toward vast fields of sunflowers.

They cover miles, skimming

dunes and charred clover.

I imagine their flying from cliffs,

slipping in canyons,

climbing to eagle nests and descending again,

yet there's no way I can join

pine siskins fleeing hot forests.

All I do is draw my quilt

to my chin, wait for morning.

Pine Siskin
Photo: J. R. Woodward/Cornell

THE WATER OUZEL

Out of the side
of a sturdy ball of moss
attached to the rock wall of the river
comes the young water ouzel
schooled during its incubation
by the icy water
crashing down the mountain.

Like an old launderer over a tub
the young ouzel rocks to and fro,
its forward dip, the lowering and raising
of its head already synchronized
with the merciless stereo of the river.

American Dipper Photo : Robert Barber/Cornell

Soon a plump stubby-tailed
seasoned mountaineer will demonstrate
the dive under water,
the walk on the floor of the stream,
the capture of small fish, invertebrates --
will tease and overwhelm the young ouzel,
will chart the life-sustaining ballet
to be practiced by this teetering beginner
to the beat of the larger music of survival.

Riddled by an orchestra
that deafens its participants
to the near noiseless pad of the wild cat,
that forbids migration
and watching sunrise over the prairie,
this flexible little novice will later,
with the finesse of a Nobel winner,
stop dipping its beak long enough
to flood the terrain
with a ringing, repetitive song --
 yes, and rise above
the ground bass of the river.

White-Breasted Nuthatch
Photo: Bill Duyck/Cornell

Of all the birds which frequent both Bear Creek and Fountain Creek parks, none is as unique as the white-breasted nuthatch. If we look at its characteristics and combine them with those of the pigmy, red-headed, and brown-headed nuthatches, distinctions from other birds abound. The one characteristic these four nuthatches found in the US share is their acrobatic movement down trees *headfirst*. This feature might be thought to have few advantages until we consider how much we miss

Red-Breasted Nuthatch Photo: Jim Wedge/Cornell

going out that we see *coming back*. Most other birds travel up and naturally miss insects and grubs the nuthatches glean. Other types of maneuverability like hanging upside down under small stems, as they search for food, are also made easier by their athletic prowess.

Other features all four share are strong, woodpecker-like bills, strong feet, and square-cut short tails. They all excavate or use tree holes for nesting, three out of the four doing their own excavating; they do not migrate except in minor ways; they are so quick that one watcher says they can catch a falling nut in mid-air; the male and female of all four species look alike; they all pair for life; at least three of them visit feeding stations; and they do sometimes inhabit nesting boxes.

Habits that distinguish each of the four are even more remarkable. The brown-headed does not inhabit our region but is found in a large southeastern US territory beginning as far west as Oklahoma and stretching to the east coast. Unlike all but a few other birds, it uses a tool, taking a loose piece of bark in its bill and prying open crevices, where insects flourish.

The largest of the four, the white-breasted, most commonly seen in our parks, stakes out a territory and remains there within calling distance of a mate. The call of this nuthatch is almost harsh in its loudness and caw-like quality. This nuthatch has "floaters," those who have not established a territory, but are available to inherit an already established area, when a former "owner" dies.

Red-breasted nuthatches are unique nest builders. Both adults apply sticky pine pitch to cavity entrances, making use of small pieces of bark, not unlike the brown headed, to apply the pitch, or resin. When the young are ready to emerge, they place small pieces of fur on top of the pitch to prevent the young from sticking to it. Probably this use of pitch also discourages certain predators. This nuthatch has a higher call than the white-breasted.

While the red-breasted are more gregarious than the white-breasted, the most gregarious are the smallest, the pigmies, seen often in flocks. They measure 3 1/4 to 4 1/2 inches. They roost communally, sometimes joining groups of 160 in a single cavity to survive the cold. They prefer, more than the other three, long-needled pine forests. With excavation of holes and bringing food to the young, pigmies employ "helpers," from their flock, who, it is believed, assist greatly to insure a greater survival rate. Sociability is thus a survival tactic. The pigmies are often heard chattering and may be the most delightful to observe, due to their small size.

REDWINGS

Redwing
Photo: El Paso County
Parks Staff

The blackbird melds into nothing more distinguished than an LBB, the little brown bird, a label we give to all those small brownish flutterers we cannot identify. The blackbird's fate is similar, except to take on the somber hues of black (if male), rather than brown. At worst, lore has it that blackbirds were baked in a pie. A kinder version can be noted in 18th century's Joseph Addison: "I value my garden more for being full of blackbirds than of cherries, and very frankly give them fruit for their songs." Call blackbirds redwings, and our recognition level leaps up. Of the same family as orioles and meadowlarks, as well as the yellow-headed blackbird, Brewer's blackbird, and others, they take on much greater interest. Seen most often in wetlands, they are not adverse to dryer grasslands. The novice can find a red-winged blackbird within a few miles, almost anywhere.

One common avian display at Fountain Creek Nature Center is the take-off of a dozen redwings from the feeding area, all flying in formation, all banking so their red epaulets form quickly fleeting and quickly returning display patterns. Anyone ready to dismiss nature as random has not watched these flights, which surely are the envy of stunt pilots and other aviators.

Energy and tenacity are also redwing attributes. Watching a half dozen redwings taunt and peck a large bull snake to exasperation, as it glides swiftly across the nature center pond to the protection of the understory, is to know this bird's strength and again, the beauty of their movement and flashing red. As sorry as we might be for the snake, it admittedly a threat to bird's eggs and young, we cannot help but admire the tenacity and purposefulness of the redwings.

Their "O-ka-ree, O-ka-ree" ushers in spring, though some of our year-round singers probably have not just returned from the south to claim territory. The male redwing will soon flash his red epaulets as he defends an extensive area where there are mates. The mean size of his harem is five, but the number has reached fifteen. Keeping the redwing population, throughout the US and adjoining countries, at a high level (they are 28th on population charts), females lay three to five eggs, often have two broods, sometimes three, during a four-and-one-half month breeding season.

Redwings are robin sized; ours are tri-colored having a orange band that edges the red epaulet. California's are bi-colored with red epaulets only. Redwings have long sharp bills which help to keep females from being confused with other brown-streaked birds. Rather than pests out to destroy crops, redwings need applause for their harvest of mayflies, grasshoppers, and caterpillars.

When fall comes, redwings form large flocks, and many move southward. Those spending the winter at Fountain Creek Park and surrounding areas are segregated by sex; hence the group of males flying away from the feeding area at the nature center flashing their epaulets in formation. (Females also come to these feeders, but they are not colorful, are more easily confused with other brownish birds, and, in my observation, do not fly in formation.)

If in flight a group of male redwings are tilting in correspondence to the velocity and direction of the wind, we can only thank these mysterious, unseen currents for a grippingly kinetic sight. And wonder at the inducements that prompt these male birds to seem consciously aware of their beauty.

THE SPOTTED TOWHEE

The rufous-sided towhee (now called the spotted towhee) is to the foothills of Bear Creek what the mallard is to the wetlands of Fountain Creek. Perhaps, this is too easy. Bird counts at Fountain Creek have listed as many as fourteen towhees and Bear Creek fifty. More often than not, however, fewer than fourteen are seen at Fountain Creek and seemingly more than fifty at Bear Creek.

Since I began walking the trails at Fountain Creek in 1992, I have seen only two. At the feeders at Bear Creek, there can be six or more coming and going during a three and one-half hour stint of volunteering at the nature center reception desk. Their calls are some of the most frequently heard in the park. In spring, they are everywhere. Virginia Marie Peterson's map shows them breeding along the northern border of Colorado and north through Wyoming and Montana, but they also breed farther south and are present year around in California and Mexico. Their migratory behaviors never cause us to be completely without them, as they are especially attracted to the foothills on the east side of the Rockies.

If we look closely at their colors, motions, and songs, we will be much less likely to dismiss them as too usual for a second glance. A good two inches longer than other scratchers like the house sparrow and junco, the male towhee's black head, back, and tail as well as its robin-red sides are hard to ignore. With their flashing white tail feathers, they are quite recognizable from a distance. With binoculars, it is difficult to miss their fiery red eyes.

Spotted Towhee
Photo: Greg Lasley/Cornell

After the males move north and establish territories, the females arrive. The males then court by spreading their tails and wings and joining their prospective partners in soft songs. Paired birds are quieter; unpaired ones sing on with vehemence. Once paired, the female builds the nest by herself, and the male seems to disappear until needed to feed the young at the hatching phase; then he works with vigor. When the female finishes hatching and is free to find food, the male relaxes and resumes his songs. Towhees camouflage their nests well, making them difficult to discover.

Birders may find the rufous-sided towhee's singing its most attractive feature. The male's song is a trill about a second long with a strong eeeee sound, sometimes preceded by one or two short notes. This song is heard variously as "drink your teeee," "your teee," or "teee." The alarm call for both sexes ranges from "chewink" to "meow." Towhees also have a soft, musical warble, sung with the beak closed. This sound (perhaps a contact call) occurs when they are perched in dense cover or foraging below for terrestrial inverts, dropped seeds, acorns, berries, or insects.

"Really, where?" soon surpasses "Ho hum" when we concentrate on their song, colors, scratching for food under low shrubs, and abundance in the foothills.

THE JET SET

The magpie takes off
like a teetering jet
uttering its version of tweet tweet—
a little deceptive, considering
it never intends to be the shy one.

Magpies Photo: El Paso County Parks Staff

Come nesting time, its spread
is no dwelling at the edge of the forest
but square in the middle
of the finest tree—a bundle
of sturdy twigs, a hanger where
small talk with underlings
and constitutional refueling
insure progressive advancement
toward lording it in the skies.

The magpie takes no sass, gives very little—
don't be surprised if your next governor
wears white shirts, black ties,
a tailed coat, and boots that pump him
into a welcoming wind.

If you grew up calling them spatsies, you possibly never elevated your interest in them long enough to use a more elegant label. Maybe you toyed with the notion of showing off to non-birders by calling them English sparrows, like you call starlings European starlings, and had your uninitiated listener say, "Really, honest, I didn't know we had any of those," but probably you've thought just plain sparrows (spit it out quickly) good enough for them and kept your voice-filled-with-honey for the finches and juncos. Especially will you consider it a bold challenge to warm up to these ever-present "outcasts," these "untouchables," if you remember those dozens of times when someone pulled feathers, egg shells, baby birds, and other nest attributes from eaves and gutters, the whole mess falling on the pavement to be scattered by cats and squirrels. "Dirty little sons (daughters, of course, too) of guns" may still be the best way for you to hail them.

However, if you liked what the nice lady said about settling old differences, you may have tried to love sparrows, and I don't mean all their classy cousins like tree sparrows, Lincoln sparrows, fox sparrows, golden-crowned sparrows, song sparrows, or any of the thirty-seven other varieties listed in Peterson's guide. I mean the ones which go in flocks, love any of your bird seeds, will take almost any handout, and enjoy a good many baths. They are the critters who hang around your house and at parks, grocery store parking lots, cow barns, almost anywhere, and seemingly prefer getting cold in winter to taking long journeys to warmer climates.

Whether we like them or not, they like us. Shortly after people in the Middle East settled down to farming, house sparrows clustered around them. Thinking they might control insects, Americans introduced them into Brooklyn, New York, about 1850; it took them only fifty years to be in every part of the US, especially in cities, where their populations grew quicker than they could be counted. Evidently the first ones to arrive in

Watercolor of House Sparrows by Linda Wolfe

America were of a sturdy stock and carried no diseases; a rather indelicate nature has thus been to their advantage. Certainly they have acclimated better where there are humans than several of their more high-classed cousins. Besides birdseed from the store, they eat spiders, seeds, and blossoms. They appropriate nests, especially of bluebirds and swallows, destroying eggs and nestlings.

There is a very well-meaning flock around my place all winter. They land in a shrub under my neighbor's window and then come over, first singly, then imitatively, in twos and threes, to my seed. After they eat, they drop down three or four at a time to the water to bathe away their itches. If the water happens to be frozen, they peck at the edges and sip the slightest bit of melt. I am thus constantly assured that life goes on outside my window. If house finches vanish, I am providing a private banquet for sparrows, with an occasional Cooper's hawk coming in after a sparrow lingering over my provisions dangerously long. In the absence of other small birds, you can get them to rise a good many rungs on your ladder of love.

Ponds in Fountain Creek Regional Park play host to the regal wood duck much more often than most US range maps lead us to believe. True, two of these maps indicate small areas in northwest and northeast Colorado where they spend time, but our area appears to be off limits. Those feasting their eyes on the six specimens gracing our ponds in early fall might legitimately question what records reveal. We might guess record keepers have not caught up with the times. Ours may be part of their comeback, which is still in process. After their near extinction caused by the plume trade, the cutting of forests where they nested, and hunting, their numbers have been increasing. Nest boxes and legislation have greatly boosted their recovery.

Wood Duck
Photo: Lawrence Wales/Cornell

Fountain Creek Park's bird counts for spring and fall consistently list wood ducks. Recent monthly tabulations show them here in January, April, August, September, and October. Counting the findings in the Pueblo area, they are seen in other months as well. In 1994, wood ducks nested in the park, and ducklings were seen swimming on Rice's pond. It is true they have spurned our nesting boxes, and it is also true that we see them as they leisurely move along their short migration route of 100 to 1000 miles, taking as long as three months to complete it. Migrating in small groups, they have many stops along the way, seeming to make a love fest of their journey. With courtship beginning in early August, a mated drake may have several other drakes pursuing his chosen female, all of which he fights off, most often with success. Not noted for preferred spots, they seem on permanent sight-seeing tours.

Without a doubt, the male wood duck is a charmer with his broad shoulders, clean lines, large red eye, and the rainbow iridescence in his feathers. Glossy green and purple, chestnut, and black contrast nicely within white outlines. His slicked-back crest challenges what sheiks have donned. Floating high in the water, he boasts a very large wing span. Standing, he is positioned farther forward on his legs than other ducks. Hands down, he truly is the handsomest duck in America. The *sponsa* in his genus name, *aix sponsa*, means *betrothed*. One writer suggests he is plumed as if for a wedding. Perhaps it also suggests he is a faithful husband, at least for one year, actively pushing aside other males seeking his spouse. The female is attractive, though in duller colors, the better to hide as she blends with her surroundings when seeking protection for herself and her young. When wood ducks fly, she leads.

By far the most intriguing phase of wood duck life is nesting. Often taking over pre-sculpted woodpecker holes, when natural wood cavities are not available, the female makes the typical woodchip and down nest for as many as a dozen eggs. It is common for several other parasitizing females to lay eggs in her nest; in fact, it is estimated that around 37 percent of her eggs are not her own. When her 30-day incubation is finished, the small ducklings tumble down from the nest, or some witnesses say are carried down by the parent. Although often the nest is not more than eight feet off the ground or over water, it has been observed to be as high as 50 feet.

Capable of perching on branches as small as one's finger because of their elongated toes and toenails, the young and old have a marvelous capacity for maneuvering through heavily branched woodlands. The soft ducklings are sometimes stunned as they hit the ground, but not beyond survival. In earlier times, wood ducks nested near farms, particularly in areas where acorns, pecans, corn, rice, wheat, and millet were plentiful. Raccoons are one of their chief predators, but snakes, otters, and owls also take their toll. Their average life span is four and one-half years.

Given to elaborate preening, these eye-catchers keep old age at bay.

Mourning Dove
Photo: Johann Schumacher/Cornell

NO REQUIEM

Something besides sadness drove
the mourning dove through Pleistocene caves,
to trees sheltering saber-toothed tigers,
and over the paths of Shoshoni,
Pima, and Chippewa.
Even the gun did not reduce this
dove to sorrow.

At first too small to meet the fate of the savory turkey,
it then took on the passenger pigeon's role,
took over its fields and farms, prospered where
this bird did not. When a mourning dove fell
for a meal, a svelte sibling took its place.

Equally at home in mesquite and citrus grove,
attracted to Russian olive, Chinese elm,
and Norway spruce, it numbers high
on population lists. No, the mourning dove
has no time for endless weeping.

The dove's call simply sends a message that the circle
is complete, that it is time to begin again,
to send a brood on their trysts. The dove knows
an end is a beginning. It speaks in tones
that compel Sadness to shrink, to steal away.

A dove on every post? Now we know their enviable plan.

Wild Turkey Photo: El Paso County Parks Staff   *WILD TURKEYS*

Bird counts at Fountain Creek Regional Park frequently include a few wild turkeys. They may turn up at unexpected times going about their pedestrian business of sorting the ground cover for seeds, berries, insects, and small invertebrates. At Socorro, New Mexico, where thousands of sandhill cranes and snow geese grace the skies, several of us spotted a small flock of wild turkeys moving through low growth in their unassuming ways. Before we saw them, I thought I had walked into a spectacular nature film on waterfowl gliding in for a landing or lifting off for the cornfields, some silhouetted against gorgeous sunsets, others giving us remarkable sights as they flew low over our heads. Such power, such avian vocal cords, such grace! I was positive I was transported into a world of magic.

After hours and hours of this splendor, it was good to come down to the basic realities of wild turkeys, gobbling in a thicket. I was back to the more believable. I was back home. Wild turkeys are good solid year-round citizens, and as welcome as those neighbors who never intrude, never exhaust your patience, and always make us proud of background, culture, and historical debt to good people. Everyone remembers Ben Franklin thought the wild turkey should be our national bird.

A pair of these large, powerful birds (thirty-six to forty-eight inches high) with strong legs, spurred in the male, is an imposing sight. Looking superficially like guinea fowl with their naked heads and necks, the males have a curious thick mass of tissue on their breasts, which during breeding season swells, serving as a reservoir for oil and fat needed for greater sustenance during this time. Their plumage is generally dark with metallic reflections and feathers edged in black. Their naked heads and necks are bright red, white, and blue. As a child I wanted to run my fingers over the colorful heads of our domesticated variety to see if they were really as leathery and wrinkled as they appeared. A formidable armload, they could not be picked up without preparatory ego building and a dare. Many a turkey feather has been salvaged for ornamental purposes.

The turkey family has a fossil record back to the Oligocene period. Not native to Europe and Asia, the wild turkey's range was formerly from Maine to Guatemala. Domesticated by Mexican Indians in the sixteenth century, they were brought to Europe by the Spanish. Our domestic turkey is descended from the Mexican race of the common turkey. Their range was greatly reduced with colonization and the spread of roads and railways. Now the common turkey occurs from the eastern US to Mexico and the ocellated turkey from Yucatan to Guatemala. Considered prime gamebirds, they have been extensively and exhaustively hunted. They have made something of a comeback because of re-introduction and game laws.

The name *turkey* probably derives from its introduction into England, where it was customary to refer to foreign traders as Turks. The name came to mean a foreign bird. Domestic birds, which have been bred for their meat, exist in a number of breeds varying in color from black to white. Some doubt that there should be two wild, non-domesticated breeds, the common and the ocellated, because they are so much alike.

Turkeys are given to extensive wanderings in search of food, but are non-migratory. They are able to survive for several days without food during periods of severe cold and snow. Polygamous, the male has a courtship display which consists of expanding its body plumage, spreading its fan-shaped tail, and swelling its naked head and drooping and rattling its wing quills. All this is accompanied by gobbling and strutting. Males have been known to fight one another to death, and they may be quite emaciated by the end of the mating season, which begins in February and ends with the start of nesting in April.

The female does all the nest building, incubates for twenty-eight days, and cares for the young. Nests are on the ground and usually well concealed. Eight to fifteen creamy-colored eggs are laid, and the female is rarely persuaded to leave the nest. The young usually spend only their first night in the nest; in two weeks they can fly to low branches to roost at night. They remain with the female until the following spring. Good walkers and relatively good flyers, they go for long distances in search of food, even flying over some rivers. They do not appear to have territorial behavior, beyond that established at mating time, and communicate readily with their clucks, yelps, gobbling, and gurgling sounds.

If you take the cog railway to the top of Pikes Peak, you are likely to see wild turkeys.

BIRDING WITH A DIFFERENCE

My before-breakfast city birding in Russia with traveler Nancy Holtzapple of Lafayette, California, netted a ruddy shelduck pair, a wryneck, a pied wagtail, and a probable chaffinch in the park adjacent to the Kremlin; the black-headed gull over all canals and rivers; the European crow, the jackdaw, and the rook at a fifteenth-century rural summer palace; and the great tit, linnet, and green finch in small parks around high-rise apartments or "palaces" in and around St. Petersburg. The familiar coast gull, the mallard, the house sparrow, and the rock dove made my total fifteen and underscored an area of commonality we have with the Russians. Casual looking for the avian lent an on-the-spot naturalness to two weeks of Chekhov, the Bolshoi Ballet, the recently revealed impressionist collection nabbed during the war, and a host of other highly acclaimed artistic performances, lectures, and exhibits.

Bird in California and you'll find some surprises, but find old friends as well. I once saw a wagtail and a redwing blackbird (the one without orange yellow in its shoulder patch) at the San Francisco airport. In California, you will look twice at magpies. Ah, ha, you'll say, but what's wrong with them? Then you remember the important distinction. Colorado magpies have black bills, and California's have yellow ones.

The towhee you most commonly see will act like the one we see in Colorado, but have brown plumage with a rusty undertail and buffy throat, and be called the California towhee. Their quail will likely be the ones with the forward-curving head plume, or California quail. The varied thrush will be a nice surprise. On first seeing it, you'll think it is a handsome, sleek robin with a little extra decoration across the breast -- a band that is black in the male and gray in the female. Note also the orange eyestripe and wingbars. Peterson calls attention to its long, eerie, quavering whistled sound, followed after a pause by one on a lower or higher pitch."

There will be an abundance of some of the birds found in Colorado: the yellow-rumped warbler, the great blue heron, the titmouse. From San Diego to Sebastopol and probably farther north, there are many white-crowned, golden-crowned, and white-throated sparrows. Western bluebirds will be around little farms east of Bodega Bay. Towns in California are much better populated with a somewhat rarer find in western Colorado: the mockingbird.

White egrets are more plentiful in California than Colorado. Hawks and vultures also are frequently seen overhead, and around Davis, there are roosting spots for many kites. Seashores and inlets furnish more than one species of loon and gull, as well as brandts, frigatebirds, scoters, oystercatchers, and turnstones. Along with these, there will be the more familiar godwits, willets, sanderlings, sandpipers, and most of the winter ducks of Colorado, including ruddies and buffleheads. I saw a lone white pelican near Malibu. Down the coast to the Sea of Cortez, brown ones seem prevalent.

One of the more interesting woodpeckers in California is the acorn woodpecker. A casual in Washington, Nevada, Wyoming, it doesn't often venture into Colorado. In family groups in towns, oak woods, and canyons, it shows off a red, yellow, white, and black head plus white rump and wing patches. Many trees of numerous varieties, including palms, show scores of holes where they have hidden acorns in the bark. California also has our more common downy and hairy woodpeckers.

Just as Anna's hummingbird is peculiar to California, so is the hermit warbler. Stay longer to see them.

SOME CONFESSIONS ABOUT WATER

Sheer terror is what I experienced on a white water raft in Costa Rica. The same would be said about a walk I took in flood time on a railroad bridge over the Missouri River. You couldn't beg me to go swimming. Why would I choose to write about water?

Driving Highway 25 several times a week and looking in the direction of the Fountain Creek Regional Park, I was never convinced there was anything of interest there. Probably it was just a flat place with a few willows. It took considerable walking in the park for me to fall in love with it, and that first occurred when I stood compulsively watching the water pour over the slanted wall by the regional trail where the irrigation flow separates into its own channel. My romance was the proverbial one which begins in anything but love and ends in a way never predicted.

A frosty, still morning with ice along the sides of the creek and sounds carrying very well helped precipitate this park's conquest. About to walk north on the trail, I heard a mallard downstream let go with a very distinct and loud quack, only to be answered by another upstream. I was positive they were communicating. Their calls were sharp, crisp, completely pure. Even the sound of water fell away. Or, at least, I thought it did.

The camaraderie of these two ducks spelled, I imagined, what I began to feel for this particular spot. You may think I am compulsively drawn to what I fear most. But I am not alone in being drawn to this area. A visitor came into the nature center with her son who was about seven. She said he'd been begging her to bring him to see the "waterfall" he'd seen there earlier. Of course, his waterfall with its modest six foot splash-down was exactly where I had become enamored of Fountain Creek.

My favorite place to start a walk at Bear Creek Regional Park is, as previously noted, along the creekbottom trail. Once I saw a chestnut-sided warbler there. It is also a good area to look for a vireo in spring and a white-breasted nuthatch in winter. If you go far enough, you'll see a Steller's jay. I often think of the great blue heron which made the journey all the way up Bear Creek following its contours exactly. Start there looking for the first pasqueflower and continue looking all summer for flowering trees, dogbane, and penstimmen. With Bear Creek's cold water, we always envision those cold sources up high, where the incline is steep and the water crashes down. Visions of water ouzels dance in our heads. There is no other sound that matches a flowing creek.

Perhaps part of the lure of creeks and rivers is that they appeal to so many of our senses, some quite subliminally. We respond to sounds whether a trickling stream or a rushing cascade. The kinetic appeal is also very strong as we experience an unconscious floating, swimming, wading, or movement associated with water. Our eyes are drawn to its movement because of the interesting patterns in the ripples and eddies. We watch for what the sunlight can do to enhance or alter the colors reflected in the water. We watch for the shadows and reflected plant life. We know that wildlife often come to drink; thirst and something close to salivation may occur. Water has a freshening effect and may encourage our sense of smell. Running water lets us know that there is an active world out there, whether we think of a lazy river or water's relentless movement forward with all its symbolic overtones.

Fascinated by something that under certain circumstances scares us out of our wits, we celebrate our capacity for change, something that is bound to happen as we explore one aspect of nature after another. What frightened us, disgusted us, or even what we believed did not exist adds a new and altered dimension to existence.

THE WINDHOVER (Kestrel)

Hover-hunter from Alaska
to Tierra del Fuego,
the windhover bullies the elements
over pastures, plains, deserts.
Steep canyons, broken cliffs, posts
and high wires all are resting places.
Holes in trees and rock formations
shelter its young.
The one I saw this morning
had an eye as intense as an ignited fuselage.
I flinched, as it lifted its tail,
beat its wings, dived toward a boulder.
Before I could blink away its grip,
dangling from its beak like spittle
was a gray mouse, its head,
already battling enzymes.

VI. THE SEASONS

VARIATIONS ON ASKING WHEN

Chocolate earth, the stained snow
under your scrub oak is shadow boxing
with roots and rocks, dreaming of seeping
down to shallows.

Your fir trees sprint up mountain,
fling their lace at caramel sky
their whiplash shouting 'hold it'
to the trickle down, their bark dry
and shrinking last year's girth.

Awaiting charter flights, white-throated sparrows
join a cautious sing-in.
Sprouts kick, restive for a nitrogen rinse,
grunting justice, justice, as old tunnels
go for outlandish bids.
Thunder tees up for a Las Vegas holiday.

Clouds play their teasing game softening train whistles.
The sun stays in its throat, roll-calling species,
coddling aberrations.
Spoiling for May rites, Spring rolls tarnished dice,
warns ice to practice disappearance before summer,
applauds its creep inward, its seductions by the South.

Winter punches dummies,
practicing old fisticuffs with April.
We wait.

IT'S HERE

I welcome this renewal, this season
of uniqueness, this time when, after many trials,
we finally get our world just right.
As I labor over these lines, thinking
they say exactly what I want them to say,
thinking they say nothing ever said before,
that they hold all the wisdom I'll need
through August with its harvest of wines
and apples to be stashed for the fall,
I forget that spring and all its expansiveness
makes me into a sapling flexing its upper branches,
causes me to pump up the energy
to look for warblers behind the hill.

I wave my arms overhead, clap
at a marauding mosquito, throw
my shoulders back, opening the way
for warm breezes, the waywardness
of thunder and the rush of rain.
Words in spring are only a prod
for rising off my duff and studying the plains.

SUMMER

Only goldfinches are still nesting.
The male may even be flashing
his spasm of color with wings folded,
then sweeping up with wings outstretched,
hoping a female will answer his signal,
knowing that he will drop to feed her
from a harvest soon to be at its best.
Cicadas percussion
while their nymphs slip
their cases on tree trunks
and shrink down to entomb themselves
until July returns again.
Committed to other ecstasies,
girls pack dresses suitable for summer,
move their legs with little concealed,
their arms freckling as they reach
for a high flying pitch.
Seeds ooze from plump clusters
onto soil needing a rest.

HELP FROM THE OUTSIDE

Just when I think the warblers
have flitted their yellows
beyond the Rio Grande
and left my backyard
to the shrinkage of winter,
the juncos, those spots of slate
pink, buff, rust, rufous, black
focused for me by white outer tail feathers,
come in a fleet.

Little pioneers, survivors, they are
sorting through my half-chewed leaves
shouldering a willow twig
to make head room

to sight lettuce and dill seed—
They never give me
their loose musical trill on one pitch,
just a few twittering notes,
and I cannot expect to find
their hair-lined cup with spotted eggs,
but any suspicion
I live in undiscovered territory
expands my vision
makes my migration inward
less of a trip.

THE LURE OF FALLING SNOW

    A walk in falling snow may remind us of an innocent bride decked out in the most delicate of gowns. As if by magic, not just the landscape but all living things are transformed. Our senses take a holiday from tallying the gouges we've made in the terrain and bask in a delightful cover-up, as if we think it will last, as if we are on the verge of a pristine and permanently new world. Not seeing varied colors, everything is richly simple until we realize we have a myriad of new shapes and patterns to contemplate. And when a flake stays for a moment on our glove, we behave like we've caught up with perfection. For a change, Beauty has given Time a thump on the head, and is taking over. What a chance to imagine nothing is flawed! And that we have no cares beyond marveling at the beautiful.

    The snow under our feet is variously patterned with tracks -- who are all these creatures out braving it? Are they enjoying it as much as we are? -- a good question to ask a bigger flock of juncos than we've seen before. Is that a fox slinking through the trees, the one we haven't seen since last spring? And what are those mallards doing out of the pond? A few minutes ago these wild things were making the tracks on the snow at our feet. Looking back at our own marks on the white blanket, we feel closer to all the live creatures for having walked where they walked. We suddenly know the animals are there, like they haven't been for weeks, as if they are claiming the special silence all for themselves. Has the snow unhoused them, make them more daring? Or does the lowered ceiling make their world more discreet, more enticingly comprehendible?

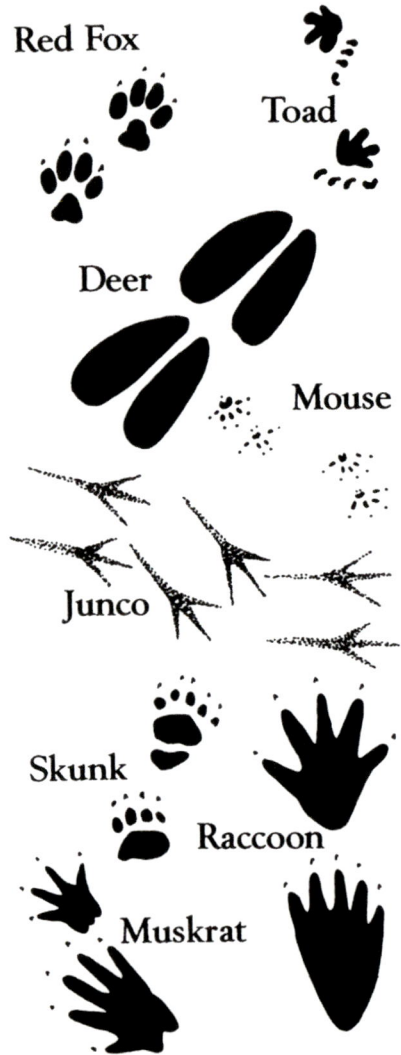

Sketch of tracks by Linda Wolfe

Just as new energy penetrates the wild world, so it penetrates us. Perhaps this energy is initially triggered by an urgency that says food may not be easy to come by, but urgency it is, establishing a moment which causes excitement to breed on itself. The heat generated by excitement is precisely what is needed to survive in the damp cold. Obviously, something is contagious because so much life is ready to celebrate, frolic. Humans even roll in the snow, make loving snowballs, and walk on forever, letting others, who wonder where they are going, go hang. The falling snow gives us the special gift of getting closer to everything that lives in the out-of-doors, to life beyond ourselves. The falling snow may even give us a chance to marvel at other creatures which do not have the option of regulating warmth with an extra sweater or two. We realize they have stamina beyond ours.

GIDDY

Resolve is in its teens.
Gone are wranglings on ice.
After winter's fleece we are flush again.
Green canopies hide intimacies—all
birds fly toward nativities. Backyards
strut. Lawns say boo, I'm here.
A rabbit sitting her fullness
capers at the thought of being
light again. Inside goes outside.
Heads reel the panoramic:
children dot pristine landscapes
gathering baskets of eggs.
Megaphones in amphitheaters babble
sweet nothings—no more blizzards,
no mass pile-ups, no influenza.
In mountain valleys
spring knights wood nymphs,
promotes geese to czars.

YOU MEET HIM ON THE TRAIL

He has a laugh that starts ah ha ha ha
then soars off in search of a thermal current.
 I met him today as I looked
for a shoveler among a flock of geese.
He told me how he wished
the white pelican would come back.
He said last year he watched it
move ten feet, flap its wings, rest,
then move twenty feet, flap its wings, rest.
A day later he saw it fly the length of the pond.
He waved his arm round and round,
rising on his tiptoes, lifting as he spun,
just as the pelican did the day it took off.
Before laughing that laugh of his, he said,
"I wish the pelican would come back,
bring the w h o l e family."

NATURAL SEIZURE

A three-year-old girl steals into our midst.
Curious, she sits to level with a turtle.
The naturalist crouches to level with her.
They name head, feet, tail.

Charging into their midst, the child's father
stops abruptly, leans against a tree, to wait
out his child's bravery. The child's eyes
dilate. She cannot leave the turtle.

Lost to what she sees,
alone in a new kind of house, she rubs
her belly to see if it too is hinged.
Turned over, she hears no one saying,
don't throw your legs in the air—
This, she thinks, would be the best house.

In three minutes her mind is back
in its hamper. Running to her father,
she tugs at his legs, is picked up, kissed.

LEGACY

Storms begin their rub
when we are womb-bound.
They hone us down
as we question the sky.
Clouds lifting over mountains
move out into the plains
to envelop and limit our scope.
The splotches of dust
the lightning catches
in a rainwash of motley
bathe us in the significance of sand.
Hail bouncing off sills
teaches us the flicker of dance.
We toddle into sense
tormenting a flower,
skidding on ice.

Children visiting the Park with Dodie Hiatt
Photo: El Paso County Parks Staff

Cover Photo Credits

1. Front Cover Photo:
   Sandhill Cranes by Charles H. Smith

2. Back Cover Photos:
   Released Into the Wild by Beth Ann Bassein
   Photo of Beth Ann Bassein by Annemarie Garza